# SAN DIEGO ZOO, PLAN OF ANIMAL LIFE STUDENTS

## May Form Society to Support Large Collection

DRS. HARRY M. AND PAUL WEGEFORTH are interested in the promotion of a zoological society for San Diego, which will have for its object the development and support of a zoological garden to be maintained out of the funds that the society will raise through dues and subscriptions.

There are a number of physicians and scientists such as Drs. Baker, Thompson, Gregg and Archie Talboy in this city and county, who are interested in the study of animal life and, it is proposed to combine them in a nucleus which will later be developed into an efficient organization.

"We already have a good start," said Dr. Harry Wegeforth, "in the collection we have at the Exposition. The cost of maintaining these animals is not large.

"There are tons of animals from Mexico, Central and South America, coming through our port and being distributed among cities like Chicago, New York and San Francisco. These animals are gifts. Why can't we keep some of them here? Zoological societies trade animals with each other and we can do the same thing when we get a surplus of any one species."

# WILD IN THE CITY
*The Best of ZOONOOZ*

# WILD IN THE CITY
## *The Best of ZOONOOZ*

Robert Wade
Editor

Marjorie Betts Shaw
Editor, ZOONOOZ

A San Diego Zoo / Wild Animal Park Publication

Zoological Society of San Diego
P.O. Box 551
San Diego, California 92112

Photographs: Unless otherwise credited, San Diego Zoo photos – Ron Garrison, photographic supervisor; F. Don Schmidt, photographer; Ken Kelley, photo technician.

Frontispiece: Indian peacock (*Pavo cristatus*)

Murals: Mural art from entrance to the Warner Administration Building at the San Diego Zoo by Tim Reamer.

Publishing Consultant: Luster Industries
Art Director: Martin Welling
Production: L. Ortiz Art Service

Standard Edition:
    Library of Congress Catalog Card Number: 85-51709
    ISBN 0-911461-12-4

Limited Deluxe Edition:
    Library of Congress Catalog Card Number: 85-51710
    ISBN 0-911461-13-2

Printed and bound in the United States of America

Print Number    6    5    4    3    2    1

# TABLE OF CONTENTS

# PREFACE

For sixty years ZOONOOZ, "the same backward, forward or upside down," has recorded the history of the San Diego Zoo, and for fourteen of those years of the Zoo's sister institution thirty miles removed, the San Diego Wild Animal Park.

The people who wrote the articles and took the pictures for ZOONOOZ were probably not conscious of recording a history. They saw the new magazine as a means of bringing to our members news about the Zoo, its people, animals and the wild places that produced those animals.

Reading through the over 600 issues of ZOONOOZ that have been published since the first one in 1926, one becomes conscious of both changes and omissions.

One notable change was mechanical. In 1966 we began the transition from black and white illustrations to the colorful magazine that is characteristic today. A man named Carl Switters gave a donation specifically for that purpose, and has provided more since to keep the color going. The results, most everyone agrees, have been spectacular, particularly since so many pictures have been taken by our great nature photographer, Ron Garrison.

As the Zoo matured so did ZOONOOZ. For one thing, articles became more professional and sophisticated, in part because authors were paid for their work after 1979, but more importantly because social attitudes about the roles of zoos underwent a change.

In the beginning our Zoo, like most others, was seen primarily as a place that provided fun and a little education for the family, most especially the kids. Over the years this role has remained constant, but others have been pushed to the fore. ZOONOOZ has revealed an increasing emphasis on education, both in the sense of classroom presentations, special tours, interpretive material at exhibits, and, of course, in the magazine itself.

Noticeable also has been a marked increase in the number of words and pictures about conservation, reflecting the rapid depletion of wild animal and plant species, particularly in the tropics, and depicting the enlarging role of our Zoo and Wild Animal Park in the breeding of some threatened and endangered species, and in the research required to do that breeding.

This increased concern about the need to preserve many wild animal species is one of the most significant changes reflected in ZOONOOZ. Before World War II, when the threat to wildlife was not so readily apparent, the editor of ZOONOOZ thought nothing of running an ad for a local furrier which showed tigers and leopards among other sources of pelts. It is a mark of our change in attitudes that displaying such an ad would be unthinkable today, even if ZOONOOZ took advertising.

As a record of our history ZOONOOZ has one outstanding deficiency. It virtually never depicts failures. Successes are always shown, because editors quite understandably tend to accentuate the positive and eliminate the negative.

In this book—the best of ZOONOOZ—this tendency is even more pronounced. Consequently, in the name of honesty let us enter into the record here the fact that we have had some failures, and dwell no more upon it.

The task of selecting material for a book that purports to "the best of" is extraordinarily difficult. Our editors have gone about it bravely, recognizing that the articles and pictures included reflect what we were at various stages of our evolution, and that space in the book would have to be found for great pioneers or innovators like Dr. Harry Wegeforth, "Si" Perkins, and Dr. Charles Schroeder, even though they wrote few articles for ZOONOOZ. Fortunately others like Belle Benchley, Charles E. Shaw, and Ken Stott were much more prolific. They made selection difficult by being uniformly good.

The bottom line is that we have material left that would fill at least two more books of this size—and what is presented here has been carefully condensed and edited to eliminate irrelevancies, outdated references, and words or phrases that probably should have been edited in the first place.

We hope you like WILD IN THE CITY. It comes to you not only as a long-discussed labor of love, but also as the first of what we hope will be many books that will serve to inform, educate and delight our members and the large public of animal lovers who visit our zoos.

Sheldon Campbell
*President*
*Zoological Society of San Diego*

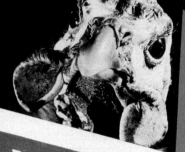

# The Zoo

## By Belle J. Benchley

*Belle Benchley, who came to the Zoo as a temporary bookkeeper and remained to become its director, set down this statement of principles in 1934. Over a half-century later, it is still the Zoo's guiding philosophy.*

**1934 Annual**

Man has always associated with animals for his own pleasure and profit, yet it has remained largely for those interested in maintaining zoological collections to become interested in and to promote the welfare of the animals themselves.

Early man enticed wild beasts by lures or captured them by force for his needs and selected those which seemed best for his domestic use. For centuries this process of selection went on while he used those which he did not domesticate for food and raiment and covers for his shelters. He kept them for companions and worshiped them as gods. The ancestor of the modern zoo flourished during early Babylonian history, through the rise and fall of the Pharoahs in Egypt and the gladiatorial combats and animal exhibits of ancient Rome. When Cortez conquered the Aztecs, he found a flourishing collection of animals and birds, which must be acknowledged as the first American zoo.

During the past century, zoos multiplied and flourished in all civilized countries. They are acknowledged to be as necessary to the best interest of a community as parks and playgrounds, which are no longer luxuries in our complex civic life. They have, in fact, become an essential part of our culture and scientific scheme of living.

While the first function of every zoological garden is entertainment, a tremendous amount of practical knowledge is obtained while in the pursuit of pleasure. In addition, through zoological societies, most of the practical work in conservation of wild animal life has its inception, so much in fact that many of the rarer species of bird and beast which have been threatened with extinction owe present existence and probably future to the study of their life habits and care in zoological gardens.

It may be true that greater pleasure and profit may be derived from the observation of the wild, but unless augmented by the more intimate knowledge to be gained in captivity, is

*The original zoo on Park Boulevard.*

seldom of much avail in scientific work. And for the comparative few who have the opportunity for extensive travel, there are the millions whose only touch of nature is to be had at the zoo.

So zoos have come into being in every small city and town. In the great centers of population, zoos are things of the greatest civic pride and the center of interest for travelers. They are, moreover, one of the greatest advertising features any city can have, for stories of animals are always news that can be worked up into attractive stories for periodicals and lend themselves to motion pictures. Rivalry exists among citizens in various communities as to the size and excellence of their zoos, but zoologists themselves appear to rejoice in the success of other organizations and attack their own problems with great zeal because other societies have been successful in overcoming similar handicaps.

The trend away from menageries and toward natural habitat enclosures for zoological specimens has been marked during the past twenty years, and from the exhibition standpoint the change during that period has been great.

Our own zoo in San Diego has for its unit of exhibition the family group and in this particular seems to be unique. The large territory encompassed by the Zoo, the simplicity of the enclosures and the ease with which the heating problem can be surmounted has tended to increase success in keeping wide varieties in family groups.

The most successful zoos are those which are under the control of a zoological society composed of men and women who have for their greatest interest the development and operation of a successful zoological exhibition for the public good. There can be no reason except scientific and philanthropic interest that motivates such an organization for there is nothing to be gained except the public good. The society serves the purpose of protecting the zoo from the ups and downs of political favor, and controlling the collection, the policies and management. The care of wild animals must be constant, scientific and untrammelled by political preference. There has been no zoo successfully maintained through long periods at its highest efficiency or serving the greatest public good except it be guided by a well organized-society.

# Doctor Harry As The Zoo Staff Knew Him

## By Belle J. Benchley

*The San Diego Zoo was created in the image of Dr. Harry M. Wegeforth, its founder and for twenty-five years its driving force. Upon his death in 1941, Belle Benchley, then director, collected a few reminiscences about this by now legendary figure.*

**July 1941**

Doctor Harry Wegeforth was bound to put out a zoo paper, be it ever so small and humble. The name he coaxed from W.B. France, who was then writing a weekly column in the San Diego Sun called ZOONOOZ. Doctor copyrighted the name at once and the first issue, a six by eight double sheet with much big type to fill the place of little news, appeared in 1926. He felt it was something fine to have a regular periodical, not a scientific bulletin but a newsy little paper regarding the affairs of the Zoo.

As for the Zoo, probably no one in the world ever built so much, so well, out of such complete nothingness. No one who has not worked with the Doctor day after day, and year after year, could have a full appreciation of the discouragements he overcame or of how he "twisted and turned" to make the most out of every possible bit of material or small amount of income.

He frankly admitted that his primary interest was in seeing the Zoo completed and the cages well filled. He employed the best people he could afford to care for the specimens and except in time of emergency held them responsible. He was always ready for a call, however, and one Sunday afternoon when a huge Indian python, climbing in a tree in a reptile cage, tore a large hole in its side, Doctor Harry, in response to our frantic calls, rushed over with his emergency kit and sewed up the tear with as much interest and skill as he would have exerted to save a human being.

He built up the animal collection by using the things he had at hand, seabirds, snakes, seals and small local animals, offering them to dealers and zoos and getting in exchange specimens which we never could have raised the funds to buy.

Perhaps funniest and most characteristic of

Doctor Harry was the story of moving two elephants through town by him and Harry Edwards, then superintendent.

The elephants had been brought in a freight car from San Francisco to San Diego and arrived stiff and weary from the long trip across the Pacific and down the coast. They were unloaded off the car in the freight yards. Doctor and Edwards stood, faced with the responsibility of getting them home, looking from the elephants to each other. It was about nine o'clock at night.

Suddenly, Doctor Harry laughed and said, "Harry, did you ever ride an elephant?" "No, but I can," replied the head keeper. "So can I," agreed the Doctor.

The two of them sat a few minutes experimenting with methods of indicating their desires to the huge beasts. Then Doctor kicked Empress behind her ears and the patient creature started forward with Queen at her heels.

Up Fourth Street to Laurel, across the bridge and into the Zoo the procession stumbled along in the darkness. Nothing happened to mar the ride, probably due entirely to the weariness of the beasts. The gates of the Zoo swung wide and the two stalked through.

Just as the Zoo is full of animal stories so is every cage, grotto and pen filled with his dream, and his energetic attempts at building, often without the fundamentals in the way of material and engineering skill.

The hills of Balboa Park were searched for seedling trees to be transferred to the zoo. On rainy days he delighted in riding around the city hunting plants and seeds he could obtain to scatter through the Zoo grounds.

The Hospital department and the research work was a natural outgrowth of his study of medicine and the work he and his brother, Doctor Paul, one of the original Board of Directors, hoped to do together. His determination to carry on has kept it alive through some very discouraging and fruitless years. He never lost sight of the contribution that the Zoo could make to science and medicine and kept on until he found finally the proper men and methods by which it might fulfill its destiny.

The vision he shared with each one of us and in everyone he left a sense of obligation to an ideal. This was well expressed by a former employee, who said, "He did more with nothing from scratch than any one I probably will ever meet."

*Facsimile of W.B. France's original ZOONOOZ column.*

---

TUESDAY, AUGUST 11, 1925

Our Motto: "The Same Backward, Forward or Upside Down"

Published Every Now and Then

# ZOONOOZ

W. B. France Editor-in-Chief

Price, 5 minutes.

Balboa Park, San Diego.

## Grand Midsummer Pictorial Number

Zoonooz takes pleasure in presenting its first grand midsummer pictorial number—the first and only thing of its kind ever attempted. If this unique undertaking meets with a favorable reception, it may be established as a regular sesquicentennial feature.

### ENGAGEMENT RUMORED

—Photo by Averett

"We are merely encaged—but not engaged." With this statement both Alaska J. Huskie and Miss Cordelia Cougar denied high society gossip that Cupid had been busy with this invincible twain. "He's a good musher, and I admire him as a gentleman friend, but he growls too much for a life companion," Miss Cougar declared.

"She's a nice girl, even if she is a little catty," Mr. Huskie confessed, "but she's too wild for me!"

❖ ❖ ❖

### OF COURSE THEY DO!

"Of course movie actors use paint," Rudolph Valentino Bear, Zooville's famous film comedian, confessed to a Zoonooz reporter.

"Make - up is a necessary adjunct to cinema art, and a bit of paint here and there doesn't hurt anybody."

Rudy said later that his statement was confined exclusively to grease paint and drug store complexionery.—Photo by Fitch and that he condemned the use of so-called "wet paint."

❖ ❖ ❖

### FUTURE CHAMP?

—Photo by Hartsook

Exclusive photo of L. A. Phant, heavyweight titleholder of Zooville, in training for his next bout. It is rumored that he will challenge Dempsey if he can raise the necessary $1,000,000 guaranty.

"Dempsey may be faster on his

feet," the Zooville zoomer declared, "but I beat him on weight, and if I land a punch he'll never smell the flowers."

❖ ❖ ❖

### STUDIES ENGLISH

—Photo by Sensor

Tequila Concarne Peccary, who recently arrived from Mexico, is snapped by the alert cameraman while taking his lessons in English. His instructress is Miss G. G. Little of Harbor, popularly known as "Little Gee Gee."

"Tequila is a knock-out," she declared. "He is so quick he nearly takes me off my feet!"

❖ ❖ ❖

### NOCTURNE

—Photo by Shimotsusa

Exclusive photographic reproduction of the beautiful pastoral, "Zooville at Midnight," the original of which was done in metal by Line O. Typer, member of L'Academie des Chambres de Composition. It will be noted that the lack of arms identifies the star as Venus, while the fact that the moon is upright shows that it is not full.

❖ ❖ ❖

### NEW INVENTION

—Photo by Bunnell

Mrs. Mandy Lay, Sacred Cow of India, is here shown demonstrating her new invention, the pedestrian's tall light.

"Many of the roads through Balboa park have no sidewalks

for pedestrians," Mrs. Lay explained, "and there is constant danger of them being hit by automobiles, which this invention will reduce. It has already been awarded the gold medal in the Safety First contest of the Cows' Anti Corned Beef association."

❖ ❖ ❖

### SAVANT

—Photo by Mehlin

Photographic study of Mr. Robert ("Bob") Katt, writer and bon vivant, author of "The Origin of The Bob," "What Made the Wildcat Wild," and other poems. Mr. Katt is here seen at work on his latest book, "Meat Eaters Have No Pimples."

❖ ❖ ❖

### REVERSES THINGS

—Photo by Swope

"I always do get up at night, and dress by yellow candle light," says Teddibear, "and when it's day, I climb a tree and hit the hay. For day is made for sleepyheads to snooze serene in sunny beds; but when the night is black and dark—ah, then it's time to romp and lark!"

### ZOO HISTORY*

*ZOONOOZ and the Zoological Society of San Diego, here and now, extend a vote of thanks to W. B. France and the San Diego Sun for giving us the name of "ZOONOOZ." Mr. France coined this word while writing a zoo column for the above paper, and they have very generously granted us full title to it.*

# The Years Behind Us

## By Belle J. Benchley

*In 1951, the Zoo celebrated its 35th year and Belle Benchley, director for 24 of those years, paused to recall some of the trials and tribulations of the early days.*

**October 1951**

Some zoos have been the result of long planning on the part of municipalities or other governmental bodies with appropriations of public lands and money or bond issues. Others have been started by philanthropists from a private hobby and with private capital. The San Diego Zoo started because a boy who loved animals and had always hoped to see a fine zoo in his native city of Baltimore, had moved to San Diego to practice medicine and had transferred his ambitions for a zoo in his home town to one in his new town.

Late in September, 1916, while riding down past Balboa Park this man heard some lions in the Exposition grounds roaring, and turning to his brother who was with him, he said, "Wouldn't it be splendid to have a zoo in San Diego?" With those words Dr. Harry Wegeforth started upon a program which has

*Dr. Harry on one of his daily rides around the young Zoo.*

never been completed but has given to San Diego what is everywhere accepted as one of the largest, finest zoos in the world.

Dr. Wegeforth put a brief notice in the paper asking anyone who was interested in starting a zoo to meet with him. Four other men, three doctors and the fourth a scientist connected with the Natural History Museum, met together and founded the Zoological Society of San Diego. It was nine years later that I became bookkeeper. The Zoo had been in its present location only three years, after a year of work and study in laying out a rugged, unoccupied and unimproved area as a permanent home.

The present beautiful Zoo did not look like much when it was opened for business. There was a shabby public camping ground under a few scrawny trees where the deer mesa now stands, the hillsides between were covered with cactus and brush with a few seedling gums in the deeper canyons. There were no roads or trails. The whole area was overrun with vines and shrubs and the present reptile mesa, a part of the model farm of 1915-1916, looked rather like some of the abandoned homesteads of the western prairies. All else was a natural Southern California country scene.

The Society too had grown from those original five grown into more than a hundred and was gaining membership steadily. Dr. Harry had begun his plan of selling the Zoo to the people of San Diego to get their moral and financial support, a program that lasted until the day of his death. A most important principle was that the life of the Zoo and its staff must be one of public service, not one of acclaim or self seeking. In our striving the Zoo must try to grow, not so much bigger as better.

Dr. Harry went east twice each year to observe the work in the best medical centers in order to keep abreast of the highest improvement in medicine and surgery. Every leisure moment was spent in visiting animal collections and dealers' backyards where he picked up many a treasure. Through a brief history he had been working on prior to his death we find such notes as this, "One day in the backyard of a little animal shop I found a Harpy eagle, and an Eared vulture, he didn't know what they were so I offered him $75.00 for them both and sent them to the Zoo."

To begin with, everything done at the Zoo was pretty much makeshift. Harry walked and climbed over the hills and canyons studying the contours and possibilities of a somewhat disappointing terrain. He also rode his favorite horse, for there were no roads about the tract, slowly day after day and gradually the plan for the Zoo evolved in his mind; pools and barless grottoes in canyons, hoofed stock and heavy mammals on the flat-topped mesas. It was such a practical and excellent plan that only in the most minor of details, he or others have ever needed to deviate from it.

Miss Ellen Scripps began her benefactions in 1921, with money for the fence and the first bear grotto. Since Dr. Harry had greatly underestimated the cost it was decided that the natural soil in that area would be too hard for a bear to excavate, and so the two black bears and one giant grizzly, Caesar, were moved into the grotto.

When the staff arrived next day there was a hole in the ground that you could have driven a team and wagon into, and only the fact that they were digging through a hill saved the bears from escaping. After that we never tried to save on reinforced concrete.

This was followed closely by the building of the old lion grotto. The huge flying cage for shore birds and the double tiger grotto were completed during the years 1922 and 1923, all the gifts of Miss Ellen Scripps. Then Miss Scripps gave us the money for our dams and pools. Two of these, built to scale, were miniatures of the dams in the city water impounding systems.

By 1925, we had our first foreign exchange with Australia. Late in 1926 the second Australian shipment was made, since practically everything in the first had been sold to enable us to progress with our building improvements. Such expeditions continued until the death of Dr. Wegeforth and World War II.

In 1927 the Hospital Building was completed and within a year we had it in full operation with a veterinarian heading the research department, thus founding a program which has opened up a new way in which large zoological collections can serve many sciences.

We had our share of bad days too when we had continued storms. I reached the Zoo one April morning in 1926 to find that Dr. Harry and all of the men had been there since midnight. The swimming pool in the old Indian Village had gone out and this water, with the heavy downpour, had caved in the front walls of our tiger and mountain lion enclosures.

One of our tigresses was swimming in the dark still water, and our head keeper in despair finally put down a ladder and climbed into the flood. He called her and she came whimpering and clung to him while he dragged her to safety with his bare hands. She had been tame as a baby but had long been considered dangerous.

We had California sea lions all over town. Some seemed to want to break into print and had invaded the office of the *San Diego Sun* on Seventh and B, but the most embarrassing

situation developed when three lost seals "flippered" into the police station asking for help.

Dr. Harry passed away in the summer of 1941, after having spent twenty-five years in dreaming a wonderful dream and seeing it almost entirely realized. With his tremendous interest in everything and everybody, and his equally great curiosity, he was marked for a life of adventure, even if he had to make his own world in which to find it. The doctor left a living growing memorial, not only in the physical plant he had created, but in the spirit of the institution, the traditions he had begun, and in the joy that his efforts will continue to give to millions, old and young who pass through the turnstiles.

*Original flight cage, hailed as the "world's biggest bird cage."*

*Bear enclosure: The first of the barless grottos.*

# 60 Years At a Glance

## By Marjorie Betts Shaw

*As the Zoo prepared to embark upon its seventh decade of existence, then-librarian Marjorie Shaw dug into the archives to provide an anecdotal retrospective of the first six. Incidentally, both the Zoo and the National Park Service were born the same year.*

**November 1975**

As he closed his chronicle on the formative years of the San Diego Zoo, Dr. Harry Wegeforth wrote, "The whole zoo was a gamble..."

The gamble began in 1916 following the close of the Panama-California Exposition, which left several groups of animals scattered throughout Balboa Park. With a dream to start a zoo, Dr. Wegeforth contacted four other men—his brother Dr. Paul Wegeforth, Dr. Fred Baker, Cdr. J.C. Thompson, M. C., U.S.N., and Frank Stephens of the Society of Natural History. On October 2, 1916, these men formed the Zoological Society of San Diego. It wasn't until 1921 that the Zoo was granted a parcel of land by the Park Commission, and it was 1922 before the Zoo was able to move into new quarters. On his horseback rides through the Zoo grounds, Dr. Harry selected sites that were best suited for grottoes and pools, decided which animals would be best exhibited on high level areas, and which would stand cooler

*The mirror lagoon and monkey quadrangle.*

areas. The mesas would hold reptiles, birds, monkeys, and hoofed mammals. Bears and cats would be canyon-dwellers. Hillsides were to be reserved for the most delicate and most valuable animals.

When walking through the Zoo, Dr. Harry carried a cane that had its tip whittled to a sharp point. With the cane and a pocketful of seeds, he began a planting program in the tradition of Johnny Appleseed. On all his travels throughout the years, he gathered seeds to try in San Diego. Although much of Balboa Park already had been planted by horticulturist Kate Sessions, the Zoo grounds were barren, punctuated only by desert scrub. Eventually, they were transformed into semitropical gardens.

During the early years, the normal means of financing a Zoo project was to plan the construction, carefully compute the cost, and borrow the money from a bank. Then prospective donors would be shown the fine new exhibit they might give to the children of San Diego. Much the same method was used for the purchase of animals.

To bolster the Zoo's finances, a policy of charging non-members was begun in 1923. In 1927, the entrance fee was raised from 10 cents to 25 cents. The dedication of the Zoological Hospital and Biological Research Institute in April 1927 saw the beginning of Dr. Harry's dream for zoo-oriented scientific and educational research.

The Zoo went through a succession of directors and superintendents until 1927, when the Board decreed that the Zoo would follow the practice of the London Zoo with an executive secretary working under the Board of Directors. Belle Benchley was appointed. Mrs. Benchley had come to the Zoo as a two-week vacation relief for the bookkeeper. She proved so efficient that Dr. Harry hired her permanently to assume some of his duties, the first of which was to speak at luncheons—a task she intensely disliked, but at which she soon became adept.

One of her major responsibilities was the selling and trading of animals. An unusual exchange was the weekly shipment of fleas to the East Coast for a flea circus. In return, the Zoo received cobras and kraits. Members of the Zoo staff made weekly trips to the public animal shelter to comb fleas from the coats of stray dogs. Flea shipments were suspended for a while when the animal shelter ran out of fleas, forcing Mrs. Benchley to comb her pet Springer Spaniel for any fleas he might be able to contribute.

Frequently the Zoo augmented its collection and its income by capturing and selling California sea lions to other zoos and circuses. Also used as exchange items were lion cubs,

*Lions Club members help dedicate the lion grotto.*

white pelicans from a rookery at the Salton Sea, and snakes found on the Zoo grounds. (The Zoo's first exhibits of snakes were those collected by workmen at the Zoo.)

Dr. Harry traveled extensively and always managed to acquire mammals, birds, reptiles and plant seeds for the Zoo. In 1935 he visited the Philippines and the Dutch East Indies; in 1937 he made a trip around the world; and in 1940, the year before his death, he traveled to the Orient. In between these major excursions he and other members of the Zoo staff accompanied Captain G. Allan Hancock and Captain Fred Lewis when their yachts cruised to the Galapagos Islands, the Gulf of California, and other points seldom frequented by tourists. During World War II, servicemen in the Pacific collected a number of animals for the Zoo.

Interspersed with the moments of pride are events bordering disaster, especially in the early years. In 1932, when the county assessor James Hervey Johnson assessed the Zoo $100,000, the Zoo claimed exemption as a non-profit, scientific and educational institution. A few weeks later it was announced that the Zoo would be sold at public auction. The City Council sent police to stop the sale, with orders to "cage the County Assessor if he won't allow himself to be thrown off the grounds peacefully." Johnson threatened to have the policeman arrested for interfering with a public official. Failing to get a bid for the animals, Johnson offered the Zoo as a whole for sale. With still

no bid, he announced that the Zoo was now sold to the State of California for delinquent taxes. The City Council pronounced the sale illegal as it was held on election day, a legal holiday. Later the State refused to accept the Zoo.

The Zoo shouldered more problems during World War II. Besides being short-handed with most of the male staff overseas, the keepers had to be armed with rifles in the event of an animal escape due to bombing. In order to feed the animals, the Zoo planted its own vegetables in Mission Valley, received donations from private victory gardens, and picked up fodder from local ranches.

In May 1972, the Society gave birth to a dream conceived twelve years earlier by Dr. Charles R. Schroeder, now director emeritus. In 1960, Dr. Schroeder began to plan and enlist support for a back-country breeding area where the Zoo could raise its own stock and hopefully reproduce many of the animals that had become endangered. While the struggles were not of the same nature as those of Dr. Harry and Mrs. Benchley, it was a long time before the dream became a reality. Four months before his retirement, Dr. Schroeder witnessed the dedication and grand opening of the San Diego Wild Animal Park.

If Dr. Harry could see the Wild Animal Park and the Zoo today, he would be amazed at the change and growth. Although he felt the Zoo would continue to improve, he thought it was virtually completed in 1941.

# An Old-Timer Recalls

## By T.N. Faulconer

*Tom Faulconer was one of a handful of dedicated San Diegans intimately involved with the formation of the Zoo. During World War I, he ran the institution virtually singlehanded when Harry Wegeforth and his brother Paul, both physicians, were absent on military duty.*

**September 1957**

In 1916 the San Diego city fathers were bequeathed a miscellaneous assortment of many wild animals at the close of the Panama International Exposition. They were housed in antiquated cages and pens on the east side of Park Boulevard. As I recall, there were a pair of shaggy buffalo, a hyena, a bear, a pair of eagles, a pair of lions, wolves, coyotes and an assortment of monkeys. Their numbers were soon reduced by one, for the bull bison had such a propensity for wrecking his pen and creating panic in the neighborhood that he became the *piece de resistance* at a dinner affair designed to create more interest in the Zoo.

Along with these animals the Zoo inherited a dissolute former soldier, known as "Army," who had an arm missing at the elbow. It was his job to feed and water the animals and keep the premises clean. It was my job to provide the food.

From contractors and farmers we begged useless horses and mules which Army slaughtered and served to our carnivorous beasts. Produce houses gave us their wilted, unsalable lettuce, squashed bananas and other fruits and vegetables, while the bakeries donated loaves of stale bread and cakes. Collecting these items meant getting up at dawn to visit these establishments before the trash collectors beat us to them.

Army generally slept in the hay mow back of the buffalo pen. But on one cold night he moved into the bear cage for warmth. Next morning he had to be rescued minus clothing and a considerable area of skin.

During the early days of the Zoo, while the Ringling Brothers' Circus was in town, Mr. Ringling offered us his gigantic elephant, "Mighty."

He said: "You know, old Mighty is the finest, biggest elephant on exhibition in the world today. But, aside from his advertising value he isn't worth a darn to me, so I'll give him to you. He is in his own car, chained by all four feet, and it takes a crew of men to rebuild his car every time Mighty throws a tantrum. Before we leave town tonight we'll unload him

*Dr. Harry and lion cub.*

and take him to your zoo, if you think you can keep him."

We raced back to the park to make ready for Mighty's arrival. We buried railroad ties four feet deep, two at each corner of a 12 × 8 foot quadrangle. We secured four lengths of heavy log chains to these ties, to attach to the elephant's leg irons, then a chain-link fence was erected, 40-feet square.

In the meantime Mr. Ringling and Dr. Harry were attending to the unloading of the great elephant from his car at the railroad siding downtown. Mighty was not co-operative. When attempting to release a shackle one of his keepers had gotten within reach of Mighty's trunk and had suffered a crushed shoulder which sent him to the hospital. All the work elephants of the circus, I think there were 12, were brought into play, but their efforts to drag Mighty from his car were futile. Chains, ropes and gear of all sorts were snapped. Prodding him with goads, even the use of smoke bombs were tried. But swathed in tons of chains as he was, and with men, trucks and a dozen elephants dragging upon him, all failed. By 2 a.m., when the circus train was about to pull out, we were forced to surrender. Mighty had defeated us all.

Perhaps it was just as well, that we didn't get Mighty for the Zoo, for Mr. Ringling wrote us a few weeks later that Mighty had been destroyed after a succession of tantrums in which men had been crippled and circus property worth many thousands of dollars had been wrecked.

At best he would have been a surly, morose exhibit, forever chained so closely that one step forward or back would have been the limit of his activities. He might have wrecked Balboa Park!

# Our Friend
# The Navy

## By Belle J. Benchley

*The Zoo owes a great debt of gratitude to the members of the U.S. armed forces who in the early days often aided in construction projects, helped spread the Zoo's reputation worldwide and frequently—as this story demonstrates—brought back exotic animals to augment the collection.*

### November 1931

One of the most interesting collections of animals which has come into the Zoo for a long time arrived by way of the *U.S.S. Vega* on June 18. This collection was interesting first because of the wide variety of animals and birds it contained but more because it had come to us unsolicited through the efforts of Lieutenant E.C. Spencer of the United States Navy, M.C., who had been stationed at Nicaragua and who was looking about for something of interest for himself, his wife, and his little son to do during their enforced exile in the service of their country.

In the beginning, Lieutenant Spencer expected to send up just a few monkeys and birds, but the more he came in touch with the natives and the native life the more his collection grew. Some of the things were easy to secure and comparatively easy to take care of but others were not, proving difficult prisoners and feeling called upon to wreck the patio garden in which they were kept.

Among those most difficult were the armadillos, who succeeded in getting out of every kind of crate or box in which they were imprisoned. In one night they could do as much damage in the garden as a drove of wild pigs. Another animal which proved a difficult prisoner was the Tamandua, or Lesser Anteater. With his strong claws he could escape from any box or crate, in spite of his inoffensive and gentle appearance. The crate in which he came to the Zoo was made of solid pieces of mahogany bound with steel with a hinged lid and the heaviest possible netting over every opening. In spite of these precautions the cargo officer of the *Vega* had been forced to nail more strips across the ventilators.

One of the greatest difficulties Lieutenant Spencer encountered was in depending upon the promises of the natives and upon their limited knowledge of the different specimens. They would promise him anything and either bring in something entirely different or fail to arrive altogether.

In spite of these difficulties, a formidable list of animals and birds were acquired including several ibis, egrets and heron, stone curlew, many parrots, parakeets and macaws, curassows, and some beautiful orioles. Among the animals were coatimundis, kinkajoos, agoutis, deer, peccaries, monkeys, ocelot, mountain lions, and a small unnamed cat very like the ocelot except for its diminutive size.

All of these shipments were brought up on the *U.S.S. Nitro* or the *U.S.S. Vega*. On one shipment they ran out of proper feed for the deer and the only thing on board which would tempt those finicky appetites was applesauce, so cans of applesauce were opened every day to provide sustenance.

Lieutenant Spencer had to list a great many things by the names the natives called them. This made the problem of securing permits in advance of the shipments rather a deep one and it was only on account of the good will of the Customs Department in San Diego and the Bureau of Animal Industry in Washington that these things were properly straightened out.

*U. S. Marines help feed a giant python.*

# In the Footsteps of Martin and Osa Johnson

## By Kenhelm W. Stott, Jr.

*To the generation which grew up between the World Wars, the names of Martin and Osa Johnson were synonomous with excitement and adventure in faroff lands. The Johnsons also played a significant role in the Zoo's development. This memoir was written by Ken Stott, the Zoo's former general curator and biographer of the Johnsons.*

**July 1974**

No two individuals more effectively promoted the San Diego Zoological Garden in the eyes of the world—from the status of "just another small-town zoo" to an institution of international prominence—than Martin and Osa Johnson.

The Johnsons' contribution to the Zoo's reputation began quite by chance in 1930 in what was then the Belgian Congo. They had set up camp in a misty bamboo forest in the mountains which rise from the western shore of Lake Edward. The primary goal of the Johnsons' Congo safari was to photograph the little known mountain gorilla [now believed, according to later studies, to be Grauer's gorilla (*Gorilla gorilla graueri*) see also page 62].

One morning while tracking gorillas, the Johnsons came upon two shaggy youngsters playing high in a tree somewhat separated from the main body of their troupe. The Johnson party cleared a broad area, chopped down the tree, and rushed in to net the bewildered apes before they realized what had occurred. As newly captured gorillas went, they were large specimens, each more than 100 pounds, not the tiny creatures customarily captured. The brutal manner of gorilla collection at the time consisted of slaughtering a mother and removing the infant from her arms.

The adolescent duo seemed to the Johnsons to be a pair—male and female. Their size and initial hostility made manual examination of the captives an impossibility. Osa named the "female" Congo and the "male" Ngagi, a word which meant gorilla in local dialect.

The Johnsons had obtained a permit to bring only one gorilla out of the Congo to America for scientific study. Now they had two on their hands. After protracted negotiation, they received a second permit. It contained an ultimatum that the gorillas be placed in such institution as the Johnsons felt best qualified to maintain and, if possible, breed the pair.

At the time, gorillas were rare in captivity and seldom survived more than a few months. Those which did exist in zoos were, with one possible exception, of the smaller lowland race. When the Johnsons returned to America, every zoo and circus that could afford to do so submitted a bid for Congo and Ngagi.

San Diego Zoo finances being what they were (or more accurately, what they weren't), any thought of placing a bid was out of the question. Nonetheless, Mrs. Benchley sat down at her battered typewriter and wrote a letter to the Johnsons, not about gorillas but about the Zoo itself and the aims and hopes she and Dr. Harry held for it.

Mrs. Benchley's letter must have conveyed the prevailing atmosphere and attitudes effectively, for Martin Johnson shot off a telegram that started, WILL PRICE GORILLAS TO YOU FOR FIFTEEN THOUSAND DOLLARS, a figure roughly half that he had already been offered elsewhere and well below any bid submitted. Dr. Harry raced out on a fund hunt. Ellen Browning Scripps and Robert Scripps, who had helped materially on many previous occasions, came up with the required sum.

In October, 1931, Ralph Virden, superintendent of Buildings and Grounds at the Zoo, went east to escort the gorillas back to San Diego. The next item on the agenda was a proper enclosure. The perennial shortage of funds again became of paramount import. Mrs. Benchley wrote the Johnsons to describe the cage required and again Martin responded, on this occasion with a check for $4,000.

Ralph Virden and crew constructed the enclosure in record time. It was completed and occupied when the Johnsons came west the following January to inspect their jet-black proteges. Ngagi and Congo had settled down, seemed content, and were obviously in good condition. Only a name had been changed. Because Dr. Robert Yerkes had published voluminous and invaluable material on a gorilla priorly named "Congo," our Congo became and

*The Johnsons visit Mbongo in the Zoo.*

*Martin and Osa Johnson in the bush: The photographers pose for a photograph.*

responded just as readily to "Mbongo," a contraction of Alumbongo, his original home. Although, unfortunately, both specimens proved to be males, Ngagi became the most magnificent silverbacked gorilla I have ever seen and with Mbongo drew visitors quite literally from the world over.

Martin and Osa, now confirmed San Diego Zoo-philes though not enthusiastic about zoos generally, spread the word through films, books, and lectures that the San Diego Zoo was something pretty special. Far more significant than the vital part they and their gorillas played in promoting the reputation of our Zoo was the indisputable fact that the Johnsons, insofar as America was concerned, put East Africa on the map.

Martin was born in Rockford, Illinois, on October 9, 1884. Shortly thereafter, the Johnsons moved to Lincoln Center, Kansas. A second move, when Martin was 11, was made to Independence, Kansas, where the father established a jewelry store and also acquired exclusive local franchise for Eastman

photographic supplies. This fortuitous incident culminated in the evolution of one of the world's greatest wildlife photographers. In handling and using Eastman products the youthful Martin acquired the skills of photography and employed them in portraiture, landscape, and news coverage. Independence was not to hold him for it offered him anything but independence. With ticket, box lunch, and a dollar, he set off for Chicago. There he got a job as a bellboy. Next, with $4.25, he set out for New York where he signed on a freighter for Liverpool. Enroute he tended a cargo of cattle and mules. Once in Britain, he took any job he could get and worked his way through England, Sweden, Belgium and France. Then, still virtually penniless, he headed home from Le Havre as a stowaway.

It was November, 1906, that Martin's first great adventure began. Author Jack London had purchased a 30-foot yacht, the *Snark*, and publicized plans for a trip through the South Seas. Martin applied for a place on board and received a telegram asking, Can you cook?

Martin, who could not, replied immediately, Yes, and set out for San Francisco. The Londons, the *Snark*, its captain, and its crew of four sailed first for Honolulu, then Samoa and Tahiti, and finally the Solomons. By this time, due to disease and perhaps in part to Martin's cooking, all aboard were too ill to continue, so the expedition came to a halt. The Londons returned to America, but Martin went on to Australia and continued around the world until he reached Boston the following year.

During the trip he had taken sufficient photographs to assemble a slide-illustrated lecture. Funds derived from this source made it possible to open in Independence a small movie theatre. During silent film days, a piano or organ and a singer were essential. Martin had only the piano. In tiny Osa Leighty of neighboring Chanute, Kansas, he found his singer. Throughout his life he enjoyed telling people, "I couldn't afford to hire her, so I married her."

With Osa, and income set aside from the theatre's earnings, he set off once more for the South Seas. This time he carried both still and motion picture equipment. Their arduous search for suitable material took them through the New Hebrides and the Solomons to photograph headhunters and cannibals. On one occasion they came uncomfortably close to being the main course at a frenzied tribal celebration. When their film "Cannibals of the South Seas" opened in New York, it played to capacity houses. The Johnsons were well on their way to becoming celebrities.

The next expedition brought them to Sandakan, British North Borneo (now Sabah). In the little-known interior of this densely bejungled island, their filmed subjects were primarily human (again headhunters), augmented by such shots of buffalo, monkey, orang, and crocodile as were rather easily obtainable. With this film they returned to New York. The company that distributed their films was less than enthusiastic. The public, the Johnsons were told, was weary of "savages" but eager for animal films. Martin and Osa concluded that the answer lay in British East Africa. From that decision evolved a magic formula, a glorious chemistry, that would produce the finest wildlife films to date—Martin and Osa Johnson and East Africa.

It was in 1921 that the Johnsons made their first expedition to Kenya. They bought a Ford, hired a lorry, and set out to film Africa's teeming herds. Initial results were discouraging. Heat waves made photography anytime between 10 a.m. and 2 p.m. next to impossible. Game herds avoided the Johnsons' carefully constructed blinds as if they were slaughterhouses.

Neither of the Johnsons could drive a car or shoot a gun. Both learned—the hard way. Once having mastered driving, they learned to use firearms, not merely for sport but because in the early Twenties the only way to feed a safari of a hundred or so bearers was to shoot dinner for them. Osa, from the beginning, enjoyed hunting more than Martin. But in later trips they both became completely disenchanted with hunting and eventually reached the point where they killed only for food or self-preservation. Telephoto lenses compared with today's versions were primitive, and the only way to get a good picture of an animal was to get close to it. This sometimes entailed a follow-through charge that resulted in a rhino dropped by Osa four feet from the tripod of Martin's camera, or an elephant that demolished a camera completely, or a lion that smashed the camera and almost got Martin in the process.

Foot, oxcart, and camel safaris in time gave way to automation; the Johnsons imported a fleet of custom-built Willys trucks. Later, trucks were augmented by aircraft, two specially built Sikorskys.

Throughout East Africa, trails established by the Johnsons are now well-traveled highways. Landing strips cleared for their planes are visited daily, some by safari planes, others by commercial craft. By their own figures, the Johnsons flew some 60,000 miles in East Africa and the Congo. The mileage they racked up on previous treks by surface travel is unrecorded.

The Johnsons' final expedition, during 1935 and 1936, revisited North Borneo with one of their Sikorskys and returned to the States with magnificent footage of orangutans, proboscis monkeys, and little-known tribes in the upper reaches of the Kinabatangan River. They also brought with them Bujung, a fine young orang male, as a gift for the San Diego Zoo.

Then they hit the auditorium circuit and played to the usual packed houses. Heading gradually west, they finally booked space on a commercial flight for Burbank. On January 13, 1937, the plane on which they were passengers smashed into a mountainside near Saugus. Martin survived only a day and Osa was seriously injured, both physically and psychologically.

She was to return to Africa but once. In 1940, as "technical advisor" she accompanied a location crew to East Africa to obtain background shots for "Stanley and Livingstone."

In 1953, United Press telephoned me the news of her death. I had not seen her since May 28, 1948, the day before I was to leave New York for my first trip to Africa. Tearfully, she kissed me and asked, "Ken, please give all my love to Africa." And throughout eighteen trips during the ensuing twenty-six years, I have done just that.

# Cashier's Lament

## By Marguerite Officer

*Marguerite Officer's humorous view of life as seen through the ticket window, although written 43 years ago, would be recognizable to today's Zoo cashiers—which suggests that times may change but people remain much the same.*

**June 1942**

Have you ever visited the Zoo and been met at the entrance with a belligerent glare instead of the welcoming smile to which you felt you were entitled? If so, please don't judge the cashier too harshly as this unhappy experience probably occurred on a Sunday or a busy holiday after her patience had been taxed almost beyond endurance by the idiosyncracies of Mr. and Mrs. General Public, and Junior Public.

Of course the people who cast a blight on the lives of cashiers are greatly in the minority but these few seem to multiply into thousands before the end of a busy day.

For instance, there are the standard "zoo" jokes which it seems at least one member of each visiting group must spring on some other member of his party, or upon the defenseless cashier. The common ones are: By someone well over forty, "Children under sixteen free; that's me; I'm not sixteen yet; I'm free!" Or, "No dogs allowed. Frank, that means you. We'll see you when we come out." Nothing particularly offensive but suppose you listened to the same ones over and over, every few minutes, every day, for months on end? Wouldn't you find it rather difficult to muster even a feeble, sickly grin?

There are people who tax to the utmost our graciousness which we strive to maintain at all times. The most irritating is the person who declaims in a loud voice that he has visited every zoo in the world and never before has he had to pay to enter. It's just what one could expect in California!

We never cease to be amazed at the people who profess to have traveled thousands of miles just to see the San Diego Zoo, and who nevertheless go back home disappointed—just because of the thirty-cent admission charge involved. Or perhaps they arrive at the entrance when we have already closed the gate and are trying to balance our books for the day, and are highly indignant when we try to convince them that most of the rare exhibits are put away in their sleeping quarters for the night and it would be much better for them to come back tomorrow.

My own pet peeve is the woman who asks what there is to see and when we mention the snakes, draws back in horror and gasps, "Oh, I wouldn't go near those horrid, slimy things for anything! George, dear, I don't have to look at those dreadful creatures, do I?" Most women, and a surprising number of men, seem to have the absurd idea that to draw back in horror from a snake is completely natural, and yet we know that these very people will spend perhaps an hour crowding around the windows in the arcade of the snake house, shuddering happily.

We are amused at people who come to the entrance, on a day when hundreds of visitors are going through, and ask if a lady in a blue hat came in a half hour ago. Not so amusing are those who block the entrance and hold up a long line of people while they argue over the possibility of going in free to find their little boy, who was sent in (without a watch) to see "everything he wanted"—and told to be back in twenty minutes! We explain that finding a small boy among several thousand people in a 100-acre maze of canyons and mesas and buildings is like looking for the proverbial needle in the haystack, but this explanation falls on deaf ears.

The manner in which a customer approaches the ticket window sometimes presents a vivid picture of the general character. There is the timid man who sidles hesitantly up to the entrance, cautiously deposits his money on the shelf and gazes expectantly at the cashier as though hoping to be spared the painful necessity of speaking. From him we must gently extract the information needed to get his party through the gate. Quite a contrast is the man who stomps to the window, smacking down a dollar bill, and shouting "Gimme three tickets, sister!"

Junior Public's misdemeanors at the gate are usually confined to running in and out and swinging on the turnstile, thus risking his neck and trying the patience of the cashier. If she asks Junior to refrain from using the equipment as a playground, Mama will resent the impertinence but if Junior gets hurt, Mama will undoubtedly sue the Zoo for negligence.

Another problem is presented by the small boy who brings his dog to the Zoo, not realizing that we cannot allow dogs inside, and the lady with the Pekinese, who insists that her tiny little dog couldn't possibly hurt our animals. We explain that the smell of a dog sets the animals in an uproar whether they can see it or not. She either leaves in a huff or talks us into keeping "Snookums" in the office, where he howls unceasingly until she returns.

*(opposite page)*
*White tiger*
*(Panthera tigris).*
*Photo by R. Van*
*Nostrand*

*(upper left)*
*Proboscis*
*monkey (Nasalis*
*larvatis).*

*(upper right)*
*California sea*
*lion (Zalophus c.*
*californianus)*

*(below)*
*Francois's*
*langur (Presbytis*
*francoisi)*

(above) Douc
langur
(Pygathrix
nemaeus
nemaeus)

(below)
Wood bison
(Bison bison
athabascae).
Photo by Hal
Reynolds,
Canadian
Wildlife Service

*(above)
Jaguarundi
(Felis
yagouarundi).
Photo by R. &
Mary Van
Nostrand*

*(below) Lowland
gorillas (Gorilla
gorilla gorilla)*

*(following page)
Slow loris
(Nycticebus
coucang). Photo
by Richard Tenaza*

## The Zoo's Pioneer Expedition

### By T.N. Faulconer

*In later years, animal-collecting trips to foreign countries became commonplace for Zoo personnel but in 1925, they were still an unknown quantity. Tom Faulconer, who served as director during the 20's, describes his one-man trail-blazing expedition to Australia.*

**August 1943**

A t least once daily, Doctor Harry would stop at my office and we would go out to inspect our "zoo." Food for the animals we begged from downtown markets. Contractors, farmers and horse traders gave us decrepit mules and horses to provide meat for our almost equally decrepit and aged lions, wolves and scrawny eagles.

Friendly seamen brought us parrots, monkeys, agoutis, boa constrictors' and coatimundis from the South. Local citizens brought rattlesnakes, opossums, pelicans and sea lions, while the bears, lions, wolves and other beasts brought forth their kind in due course. Thus, when Doctor Harry returned after the war in 1918, we had an assortment which we displayed with much pride.

Then came the idea of an Australian expedition. We wanted strange creatures from the bush and the deserts of the Antipodes. The newly started zoological garden at Sydney and the older one at Melbourne might covet the fauna of North and Central America if only we reminded them of their need. I wrote and both cities agreed to exchange animals with us if we could arrange for transportation.

At that time John D. Spreckels was a powerful figure in the Oceanic Steamship Company and he, little realizing the scope that our enterprise would assume, agreed to provide us passage to and from Sydney.

*Union-Tribune*

*Tom Faulconer and the Zoo's first koalas.*

*Kangaroo.*

After several hectic months of assembling birds, animals and reptiles for which the Australian zoos had expressed their preference, and of building shipping crates and cages, a dozen trucks rolled our shipment to the railroad in the midst of an unseasonable rainstorm. At Los Angeles we transshipped to other cars, unavoidably permitting cages and contents to stand for hours in a cold and dreary rain while we fought to have our car attached to a train that would reach San Francisco in time.

Arrive we did, only to find that the Oceanic officials had taken Mr. Spreckels' request for transportation as a joke, and had made no preparation to carry us. Twelve hours of madly racing taxicabs, brokers' offices, irate company officials, reluctant ship's officers, stowing of crates, buying of food supplies for the three-weeks voyage and attending to the hundreds of last-minute necessities finally were accomplished. I dragged myself aboard the *Sierra*, half-starved, aching for sleep and sore in every bone and muscle—but still facing the task of lashing down the several dozen deck-stowed cages and of brow-beating the boatswain into lending me canvas and men to protect my charges against the storm that was going great guns outside the Golden Gate.

That I had a cabin I knew, and I heard the stewards announcing meals in the dining saloon, but we were half way to Hawaii before I had time to get into bed or to take my place at the mate's table for a meal. For three miserable days and nights a strong wind dashed salt spray and blue water across the deck, drenching the animals and threatening to overturn and smash the piled up cages.

With occasional help from a friendly seaman, I dragged meat, grain, fish, fruit and other food up a seemingly endless ladder to feed my traveling zoo. Between feedings there was the cleaning of cages, doctoring the sick and sympathizing with the monkeys, wolves and coyotes, every single one of whom suffered from sea sickness more severe even than I.

The fourth and fifth days out brought less boisterous weather. Canvas was yanked off the cages and all hands, including myself, enjoyed the sunshine and the almost forgotten luxury of being dry. Two or three birds and small animals had succumbed to the prolonged exposure, and were dumped overside. Others perked up and we had a grand chorus of wolf howls, monkey squeaks, parrot-squawking and occasional roarings from the big crates in which four 12-foot alligators expressed their opinion of cramped quarters.

In the bright afternoon sunshine occurred the most tragic event of the voyage. Black Billy, a spider monkey that had been a source of joy to the children at the San Diego Zoo, found a small hole in the canvas side of his cage. He enlarged the hole until it would accommodate his arm and shoulder, and he reached into a wildcat's cage to snatch a piece of meat. The wildcat snatched too, and Billy had lost an arm before I could reach the scene. That afternoon, Billy's remains went overside into the sea.

One brief but violent squall disturbed us, during which one of the alligator boxes was thrown against a stanchion and weakened to the extent that its inmate managed to escape. Screams of fright summoned the mate when twelve feet of inquisitive alligator started wandering about among the passengers who had stayed up late to enjoy the stormy tropic night. We scrambled over the ship for an hour or so before one of the crew succeeded in dropping a noose over the 'gator's head. and eventually we were able to drag the big brute back into his cage.

On the twenty-first night after leaving San Francisco, the *Sierra* made her landfall off Sydney Head and lay until morning, when we made our way through the channel and up to Circular Quay.

My first few days in Australia, much of my time was spent in the botanical gardens, a very beautiful park extending from the harbor front for a mile or so across the city.

Most interesting from the zoologist's standpoint was the Platypus Farm. I procured three echidnae, land equivalents of the amphibious platypus. Part bird, part mammal, the platypus and echidna are quadrupeds, with duck-like beaks, that lay eggs, and suckle their young which they carry in pouches.

Upon returning to Sydney, I plunged at once into the selection of animals, birds and reptiles to be brought back to the United States and into the preparation of crates, boxes and pens, food supplies and other necessities. Fortunately, there was no dickering to be done at the Taronga Park zoo. Our good friends there were disposed to treat us with utmost fairness.

Giant red kangaroos, and grey ones, wallaroos, wallabies, wombat, Tasmanian devils, dingos, native cats, tree kangaroos, bandicoots and opossums; Leadbeater's cockatoos, eclectus parrots, Mandarin ducks, magpie geese, kookaburras, emus, cassowaries, bower birds and birds of paradise, big carpet snakes, tiger snakes, water dragons, and scores of cages of Wonga pigeons, cockatiels, finches and small fry of all sorts—until the after saloon deck was packed to the top of the awning stanchions and every available foot of the main deck was filled. The captain fumed and the mate swore, but still the crates, cages and bags, barrels and bales of food came over the rail until the last lorry had left the dock.

When I had last visited Taronga Park the Australian government still had not consented to lift their ban on the exportation of echidnae, koalas and kookaburras, and the zoo authorities had not consented to part with the large king cobra that they recently had imported from Ceylon. The kookaburras had arrived, however, and my collection was a numerous and unusual one, so I made up my mind to swallow my disappointment, although I felt at the moment as if I would have traded a dozen kangaroos and wombats for a single koala.

Then, just before the "all-ashore whistle" boomed its warning, a little delivery truck whizzed up to the gang-plank with two larger crates surmounted by a big sign bearing the words:

"KOALA BEARS FOR THE CHILDREN OF SAN DIEGO, U.S.A., FROM THE CHILDREN OF SYDNEY"

A small iron-bound chest was included in this last-minute delivery, and that was taken down to my stateroom by the zoo men, who refused to deliver it to stevedores or crew members. Until my room door was closed, they refused to satisfy my curiosity, then whispered to me that the chest contained the enormous king cobra, which they feared the ship's captain would have denied admission had he known.

During the long voyage back, there was little time for social life. Before dawn every

Emu.

day cages must be cleaned. Then came the squabble with the bosun and his crew, who didn't mind drenching the cages with powerful streams of salt water as they hosed down the decks. The first morning out of Sydney, the hosemen had turned their stream against the wire mesh front of an emu's cage, so frightening the big fellow that he struggled frantically and fell, breaking his thigh.

Then there was the preparing of food for the birds, meat for the wedge tail eagles, kites and dingos; chopped Lucerne, grain, carrots and fruit for the big birds, kangaroos and their kind; fish for the pink pelicans and opossum, water dragons and kookaburras; milk and ground meat for the echidnae; papaya, mangoes, passion fruit and bananas for the Nicobar pigeon and birds of paradise, and most important of all, sponge calf milk and tender fronds of the eucalyptus tree for the koala.

I had, too, the task of doctoring the emu with the broken hip. With the aid of the ship's doctor I managed to rig up a sort of hammock in which we suspended the nearly 200-pound bird from the top of his cage. A ditty-bag containing a handful of ether-soaked cloth was dropped over his head, and we set the broken thigh, put on splints and built up a plaster cast before the patient awoke. For three solid weeks I fed the big brute twice daily by hand, pouring into his capacious maw endless scoops of mash made from Lucerne, chopped fruits and grain, only to have him regard me as a target for vicious pecks which he never failed to aim at my face whenever I came within reach. As further evidence of his ingratitude, the emu tore loose from his hammock after arriving in San Diego and further injured himself to the extent that it was necessary to kill him.

The king cobra was another casualty of the voyage. Occasionally at night I would hear him stir and hiss in the iron-bound chest at the foot of my bed. He had refused to eat at the Taronga Park Zoo, and they probably would not have parted with him had they not anticipated losing him by starvation in any event.

When we had been at sea about ten days, I no longer heard rustlings and hisses from the cobra box, so I examined him as best I could through the small air vents. He refused to hiss or show fight when I blew upon him or touched him with a small rod, and I decided he was about to die of starvation.

I had fed rattlesnakes and moccasins by force at the San Diego Zoo, stuffing raw eggs and chunks of meat down their throats. My only chance to save the king cobra was to employ similar tactics, so I took into my confidence a seaman by the name of Fisher, who had helped me with feeding and caring for the animals since leaving Sydney. Fisher didn't like the idea of handling a deadly reptile, but I persuaded him, with the aid of a $5 bill, to take on the job of holding the cobra while I did the feeding.

With cabin door locked, I carefully opened the box and quickly grasped the cobra just back of its head. He mildly resented this and threshed around for a few seconds, then quieted down and I dragged his full length out upon the cabin deck.

Finally we were all ready to proceed. I gently pried open the cobra's jaws and propped them apart with a six-inch board, wrapped in cloth to prevent injury to teeth or mouth. As if automatically, the long poison fangs appeared as the mouth was forced open, standing almost at right angles to the upper jaw.

That the cobra resented being handled was by now evident. Fisher was a brawny sailor, but he was unable to prevent the snake's head from jerking about in all directions, and the blanket covering the writhing coils heaved like a stormy sea. From the two fangs, dirty yellow venom oozed, filling the little cabin with a nauseating stench.

For the cobra's dinner I had placed a dozen eggs in a basin of warm water, so that they would be moist and therefore slide down more easily. I dropped the first one into the snake's mouth and poked it down with a rod until it struck Fisher's constricting hands, then had him slide one hand over the egg and just back of the snake's jaws, which forced the egg downward.

Seven or eight eggs had followed the first when the cobra decided that he would stand no more foolishness. With terrific writhing and a quick jerk, he threw the prop from between his jaws and closed them upon the egg that was just leaving my fingers. The contents of the egg splashed and dripped, running down the cobra's neck and over Fisher's hands until everything was slippery as grease. It looked for a few unpleasant moments as if the cobra was about to take control.

I was able, however, to drop a bath towel over the snake's head and to give it a couple of twists before Fisher lost his grip entirely. By the time we had the cobra back in his box,

*Wombat.*

*Platypus.*

both Fisher and I were drenched with perspiration, nauseated and shaking—and before we got to San Francisco about a week later, the cobra proceeded to nullify our efforts by quietly dying in his box. In the dense fog off the Farallones, where we lay for several hours awaiting a chance to enter the Golden Gate, I dragged the cobra's box out to the deck and dropped him over the side. I have often wondered whether the chest floated ashore, and what the finder must have thought when his dreams of a sea-borne treasure crashed at the sight of a giant cobra's corpse instead of golden doubloons.

Permits to land had not been arranged for. Department of Agriculture officials read me laws, acts, bulletins, rulings and regulations. Customs authorities had their say, as did various other departments. When everything else was settled, certain animals having been ordered into quarantine, others temporarily detained and examined, import taxes waived and what not, the final blow came. An inspector had discovered a chunk of half-eaten papaya in a dark corner of the wombat's cage. Papayas might be infested with the some pest, and if the animals had been feeding on papayas, other cages might have eggs of that pest or some other concealed about them,

and so it was ordered that every cage, box and crate must be sterilized with live steam before a single animal could be moved from the docks.

Obviously, cages could not be steam sterilized with birds, animals and reptiles in them, so the man from the San Diego Zoo and I started upon our heart-breaking task. Tropical animals and birds were transferred from one cage to another on the windy, rain-swept docks. We'd sterilize a cage, transfer the contents of another cage and sterilize that one. Toward midnight my helper became ill, and I finished the night alone. When he returned in the morning, I left the sterilizing job to him while I went out to arrange for shipping our cargo south.

About noon I returned, finding my assistant sick again, the job unfinished and a few dozen choice birds from my shipment flying about the docks or entirely vanished.

Eventually, however, we did get away from San Francisco, and our welcome to San Diego made up for the unpleasant days and nights we had just gone through. Even with our losses considered, we had brought back to San Diego an exceptionally fine and numerous assortment, all of them entirely new and different from anything we had in our Zoo.

# Singapore At Night

## By Harry M. Wegeforth, M.D.

*While Dr. Harry Wegeforth's contributions to the Zoo were vast, his contributions to ZOONOOZ were negligible; he was a doer rather than a writer. One of the few exceptions is this excerpt from his diary, written during a trip to the Orient the year before his death.*

**March 1940**

After dinner I took a street car to the bird store in Chinatown, about a mile from the hotel, and walked around the streets a bit, as I enjoyed watching the coolies eating their evening meal and playing games in the vacant lots.

Some of the fakirs on the street corners are very convincing and put on a really good show. One of the men was selling a lotion to rub on bruises. He, by way of demonstration, would hit his arm with a piece of iron until it left a bruise and the blow would be so hard that the iron would bend. Then he covered the bruise with a piece of colored material, rubbed on some lotion, and the bruise would disappear and the arm became normal in a few moments. He was able to cause a swelling of the arm by adroit contraction of the muscles, and of course as he rubbed the lotion into the skin he would relax the muscle and the arm would become natural again.

This performance was repeated over and over for nearly an hour. It was a clever trick, but I suspected that he paid for his deception the next day, for his arm was sure to be sore. He sold quite a few of the bottles of lotion, and as I looked at the black liquid and smelled the unpleasant odor I reflected that it should cure anything it touched by the simple power of force. There were other fakirs exhibiting cures for this and that; and farther down the street were two doctors, dressed all in white to give authenticity to their use. They were selling vials of medicine and were doing a thriving business. The rikisha men live in this neighborhood, crowded together in two and three story buildings, and they are the toughest looking lot I have seen in a long time.

While I was going through their territory I saw a girl dressed in black shirt and trousers. She was talking a blue streak and selling what I at first thought were vials of perfume but later discovered was medicine which was supposed to have magic powers. She was a good talker but I did not see anyone buying. She may have been using this method of attracting a crowd so that she could expound her political beliefs. I do not believe it is possible for anyone to take a parlor view of Singapore and really know what it is like. It is necessary to taste, hear, see, and live it in order to know the real city. There is always the heavy, almost intangible odor of incense shrouding Chinatown, and combined with the smells of cooking food and the odors of the street it is, at times, almost stifling. The Chinese burn various kinds of incense in front of the buddhas in their homes and the scent creeps into every crevice and lingers there.

More than the smell and the taste of Chinatown, there is the sound; the babble of voices, not harsh and discordant, but warm and friendly. Unforgettable is the strange, uncanny noise made by the clopping of hard wooden sandals of the Chinese workmen as they go to their jobs early in the morning. The sandals are held on by a toe band and as they hit the pavement the sounds are not unlike those made by the erstwhile milkman's horse as he made his rounds early in the morning hours.

The Chinese are considered the finest cooks in the East and do all of the cooking in hotels, as well as in the food stalls along the streets. I had always wanted to taste the ancient eggs so I went into a special Chinese restaurant and had some of them in a salad. They were a solid dark color but had a nice flavor and did not have an unpleasant odor, although the taste was completely different from that of fresh eggs. In the street stalls you can see enormous stacks of black eggs piled up like the oranges in our markets at home. They are preserved by dipping them into some sort of black mud and then allowing them to dry. I was surprised to find that most of the Chinese prefer duck eggs to hen eggs and use them almost exclusively in their cooking.

The poorer Chinese live in one room, and when this room is on the ground floor there is nothing to protect it from the eyes of the passerby except a curtain hung in the back, which shuts off the sleeping quarters. These families, crowded together in their small room, pay no attention to the people on the streets unless they see someone with a camera. If one of the natives sees you taking pictures, the word is passed along and everyone melts away. Carrying a moving picture camera through Chinatown is like carrying a machine gun for it clears the streets of everyone except the kids, who crowd around, jump up and down in front of the camera, assume poses, and make general nuisances of themselves.

While practicing medicine I had acquired the habit of sleeping whenever I could, so that now it is no hardship for me to get up at any time of night. In my travels I often sleep during the day and when I awaken after dark I go out and look around the city. In this way I sometimes see unusual and exciting scenes. The morning after my trip to Chinatown I awoke at four o'clock and, hearing the sound of wooden shoes on the pavement outside, I got up and looked over the porch to see what sort of creature was passing by at that early hour. It was a Chinese coolie on his way to work. Then I looked across the street at a third story window of a building facing the side of the hotel and saw a Chinese woman praying to Buddha. The woman was the wife of a laundryman; the entire floor was devoted to laundry work. However, this morning, with the air so still and hushed, with the candles burning brightly and the incense circling up, she looked like a lovely Chinese madonna.

Out on the street I saw a few night watchmen stretched out on their cots in front of the doors of the different neighborhood stores. I couldn't see what protection they were for they are directly in the path of pedestrians, who seem to be passing by all through the night, and apparently their sleep is never disturbed, but this morning I forgave them their indolence for they looked so at peace with the world. Somehow they were fitting complement for the laundry woman at her early morning devotions.

# In the African Bush

## By George H. Pournelle, Ph.D.

*In 1956, the Zoo sent out its first African safari under the leadership of Dr. George Pournelle, then curator of mammals, and sponsored (since finances were tight) by local automobile dealer Glenn Pearson who, with his wife, accompanied the expedition.*

### October 1956

Yesterday we spent the whole day on the Althai Plains in the Royal Nairobi Park. We counted 11 species of mammals, giraffe, zebra, kongoni (hartebeest), Grant's and Thomson's gazelles, and many more. The great herds are unbelievable, yet they are not nearly as numerous here as in some of the other places where we are going. We drove through a large troop of doguera baboons. I counted 64 and no doubt there were many that I missed. One big male came over and jumped up on the hood of the car with hand outstretched for a handout.

East Africa is a strange, beautiful country. Most people realize that one does not encounter jungle and rain forests here. Few people, though, realize how much it resembles the back country of San Diego.

During our drive into the back country I got out of the car at one of the little dongas to read a sign that was posted on a tree. It was my first experience with this harmless appearing countryside. The sign read, "Lion Donga . . . Remain in Car."

I am writing this from camp at the rim of N'Gorongoro Crater. We have just come up

*Pournelle and party pose with captured baby gazelle.*

after spending three days on the crater's floor. From the window I can see the whole expanse of the crater... a dry soda lake near the center, then some plains, a lake of water to the right, and finally a large expanse of forest (mostly yellow-barked acacia) in the center foreground.

I can pinpoint the spot where yesterday we drove up to investigate what had attracted a group of vultures that circled overhead. We found three lions sitting in the grass not far from a freshly killed wildebeest, while jackals were vying with the vultures for the remains. I also can see the marsh and pool where we counted 124 flamingos. I can almost see the old rhino that we played tag with in the jeep (we chased him and vice-versa).

I wish you could see this firsthand... the sun splashing down the 2,000-foot slopes on the far side of the crater, the dark shadows, purple and mysterious, drawing in from the sides as dusk comes on... and hear the hush of expectancy broken by the occasional yap from a jackal in the distance. It makes one say, "Thank God there are places like this left in the world."

The crater rim is 7,000 feet above sea level while the floor is 2,000 feet lower. This crater is probably the remains of what was once a large lake (12 miles across). It has, without doubt, one of the largest concentrations of game left in Africa. We saw thousands of wildebeests, zebra, and Thomson's gazelles. At night we could hear jackal and hyena break the stillness periodically. In addition we saw waterbuck, a large herd of eland, led by a magnificent bull, hyenas, both the black-backed and the side-striped jackals, lions, rhinoceros, vervets, baboons, crowned cranes, greater bustards, flamingos and many others. The animals migrate from the Serengeti Plains during the dry season.

There are several Masai tribes living in the crater. These tribes maintain large herds of cattle, both for prestige and for milk and blood which form a major part of their diet. They bleed the cattle and mix blood with milk. They also will occasionally eat one of the cattle if it dies. These boys are afraid of only one thing in the world, work. For this reason they are not looked upon with the greatest favor by the settlers. It is amazing to see a large herd of cattle grazing, tended by a small boy, perhaps 10 or 12 years old, armed with a spear—this grazing taking place very near a donga where a family of lions is holed up.

After leaving N'Gorongoro Crater we drove across the Serengeti Plains and camped in the middle of wonderful game country, about 100 miles from the crater.

The place we camped is called Seronera, a spot green and lovely because of recent rains. Antelope, zebra and lion are quite abundant. On the way in we saw three hyenas fighting with vultures over a freshly killed Grant's gazelle. The hyenas were tugging in three different directions while the agile little jackals would dart in and out, being chased first by one and then the other of the hyenas. The vultures just stalked along, waiting their chance to get into the act.

Our first night at Seronera we heard lions chanting, also the chattering of hyenas. We went looking around in the jeep next day and came upon a pride of lions. They were stalking a herd of Topi (a species of antelope). We had spotted only three but on approaching closer we were quite surprised to see the full pride gathered together. Two were males, each magnificently maned.

The next day we went back and found the same two males there, both asleep. We drove within 20 feet when one awoke with a start and gave us the dirtiest look I ever seen. When he crouched to spring we got out fast! He could have landed on our jeep in one bound.

One of the surprising things about this country is its innocent appearance. You can drive up to within 20 or 30 feet of a lone tree in a barren looking terrain and then discover a group of lions that from a distance had blended into the background.

At one place on the way south we passed through an area where a large herd of elephants must have their present headquarters—large trees were pulled down all over, and many were drawn across the road. Our guide says that this is common practice... for some reason they seem to resent the roads and try to cover them.

A large tree we passed was adorned with a skull and crossbones, with the caption: "Traveler, do you have water, food and spares? If not, turn back. You have been warned."

I have passed the word along for animals at every native shamba that we have stopped near—but so far no luck. Actually, the species that I am after, for the most part, are rather rare.

After leaving the native village of Rungwa, we traveled 180 miles south to Mbeya in southwestern Tanganyika.

Leopards are thick in this area. A native boy was killed on the day we arrived. These cats are clever and hard to find when one is hunting them in the rocky areas, where they remain during the day.

After leaving Chimala we turned north on the North Road, the main north-south highway in East Africa. Its name is very misleading... just another dusty track. So we turned off on a side road leading westward to the Great Ruaha River. Before reaching the river we made camp one night in flat, acacia-studded country... very dry.

Here we were fortunate enough to find an elephant water hole. These big brutes have an uncanny ability to smell out underground water in dry areas, using their tusks as dowsers. They use their tusks to gouge out a hole big enough to drive a pickup truck into. Usually they cover the hole before leaving, but this chap had left his open, apparently planning to return. After filling two five-gallon cans and a bucket of water from this hole it appeared as full as before, from seepage.

From this point the country became wilder... even the natives would run when we stopped to ask for information. When they could be approached the information was unreliable. They spoke of distances as so many hours of walking. At one point we asked two of these citizens how far it was to the Great Ruaha River. One said it was six hours' walk; the other said three. It took us close to three hours by car.

Our camp site on the Great Ruaha was beautiful... big trees bordering this wide, though sluggish, muddy river, with hippos playing all along the stream. A few crocodiles also were seen. At night, all around the camp, elephants would bring down large trees with resounding crashes. Each morning we found fresh signs of these fellows. Their strength is sufficient to pull down trees that are a foot thick.

Speaking of elephants, the ability of an animal the size of an elephant to conceal itself in sparse cover cannot be conceived. Herds of 30 and 40 can be in an area and unperceived until one is right among them. This gives you a very chilly feeling.

It was with mixed emotions that I prepared to leave. Though I had lived in this land for only a short time, I had come to love it. Only those who have seen this wonderful Eden can understand. As the old Arabic proverb goes, "Stranger, when you have tasted the waters of Africa, you will always thirst until you return to drink again."

# The Enchanted Islands

## By Park W. Richardson

*Park W. Richardson was sent to the Galapagos Islands on assignment for the Scripps Institution of Oceanography. While there, he doubled as an unofficial agent for the Zoo and, with an assist from the local tuna fleet, returned with a rare collection of mammals, birds and reptiles from the fabled islands.*

**October 1958**

The sun was hot—blazing hot; and my feet burned as I trudged along over the scorching rocks and sand of Barrington Island. It was one of the days on which I had gone in search of the rare land iguana; and I was greatly distressed because my helper, Ernesto Ricaurte, was in considerably worse shape than I. With two of his fingers nearly bitten off by a sea lion, he was bleeding profusely and weakening very fast. My only concern at that moment was for our safe return to our home base, San Cristobal Island, some 22 miles away.

Undoubtedly, that was the most exciting incident of my six-month stay on the equatorial islands 600 miles off the coast of Ecuador.

My principal mission was in the interest of the International Geophysical Year program. It encompassed tide measurements throughout the Islands sometimes called the Archipelago de Colón, but better known as the Galápagos. Another name often applied to the group is "Enchanted Islands," so-called because of the heavy haze and cloud structure which constantly envelopes them.

After four months, I had the program to a point where I could take a little time to travel to the other islands in search of animals promised the San Diego Zoo.

Land iguanas are much more difficult to locate than their cousins, the sea iguanas. They are near extinction on the Island of San Cristobal, so collecting was avoided there. The uninhabited islands of Hood and Barrington, however, still have quite a few land iguanas. My helper for this trip was Ernesto, an Ecuadorian naval chief. Our transportation was a fourteen-foot outboard motor boat.

We left San Cristobal Island at 4:30 a.m., headed directly toward Barrington. By the time the sun had risen we were out of sight of all land, and navigating strictly by dead reckoning. After running for three hours without sighting land, I decided that we were off course and began scanning the horizon for some sign of land. By luck, I sighted a dark island shape on the starboard bow. We had been pushed about ten miles off course by the current. It had taken us four-and-one-half hours for a supposedly two-hour trip to Barrington.

As we approached the beach many sea lions took to the water, undoubtedly scared away by the sound of the outboard. We unloaded our equipment, took a quick drink of water, and headed inland in search of land iguanas.

The first land iguana was discovered sunning himself beside one of the giant cactus trees, so characteristic of Barrington. Upon our approach he bolted off at amazing speed. Ernesto and I gave chase, and after running half a mile the iguana hid in a pile of volcanic rock. Digging around this rock pile for about 45 minutes we managed to uncover a hole above him.

Land iguanas will bite if given a chance. So, with much care I grabbed his tail and slowly worked his body out of the small hole. The squirming reptile was deposited in the burlap sack and one iguana was captured!

The same procedure was followed for the other iguana taken that morning. About midday we returned to the boat for our lunch and a short rest. Then taking up our chase again we managed to unearth four more iguanas during the next four hours.

Since we had seen no fur seals, I decided to settle for sea lions; and as we were returning to the boat we passed another beach loaded with these sea mammals. They were all sleeping soundly in the sun, so we walked among them to pick out those most desirable because of their small size. I pounced on one and Ernesto put a sack over his head. We laced him up after a brief struggle.

The next one was our nemesis. After I grabbed him and Ernesto was inching the burlap sack over his head, the sea lion twisted around violently, and all but bit off two of his fingers! The pain and flow of blood left Ernesto in a near state of shock. Cutting loose the first sea lion, I grabbed both sacks of iguanas, my rifle and camera, and headed for the boat with Ernesto.

It was a quarter of a mile away; and the underbrush was extremely thick in that area, inflicting many painful cuts and scratches on both of us during the forced march. By the time we reached the boat I was half carrying, half dragging Ernesto, all our equipment, and the iguanas. At our camp I poured a bottle of antiseptic over Ernesto's injured hand, and bandaged it loosely. Then I carried him through the surf to the boat. We were headed back to San Cristobal in a matter of minutes. The sea was rough and constant bailing was necessary. It was 9:30 that night before we arrived at home base and Ernesto's throbbing hand could be properly cared for.

*Galápagos land iguana.*

*Galápagos marine iguana.*

Marjorie Betts Shaw

Our newly captured specimens were stubborn about eating at first. But after two weeks of forced feeding, once a day, they were completely cooperative. We would hold the body with one hand and the upper jaw with the other, being careful not to get our fingers in the way of their teeth. By exerting a slight pressure behind the upper jaw, we would force the animal to open its mouth. Then the food was inserted. The iguana, aroused by this time, would clamp down on the food, thinking that it was getting a few fingers perhaps. Having tasted the food the reptile would, as a rule, chew and swallow it.

Sea iguanas were no problem as they are very plentiful on all of the islands. They grow to a maximum length of about five feet. The largest specimens are found around the north end of Isabela Island, some 72 miles away from home base.

As a rule, they lay their eggs in the cover of stunted growth found near the beach. When first hatched the young have white spots, and feed on flies and other small insects; whereas the adults appear to exist mostly on algae.

As a rule penguins are found only on the west side of Isabela. However, I sighted them at times on the Island of Genovesa and on the east side of Isabela. The Galápagos penguins are small birds which live on the rocks near the ocean. They feed on small fish. I caught them by swimming up to the rocks on which these birds were standing. I could get within two feet, then I would have to make a quick grab for them. They head for the water when frightened and are next to impossible to catch there.

On land, they are slow and clumsy and have a quite comical, hopping way of walking. They will peck you rather severely when first caught, but soon become tame.

After several trips we still had not sighted fur seals. But Galápagos sea lions were present on the isolated spots away from the settlement of Wreck Bay on the island of San Cristobal.

At low tide the animals were lying among the rocks and on the sand beaches. All were over four feet long and had to be caught by working a noose around their necks. As soon as the noose was tightened the animal would jump up with a snort. Another line was worked around the rear flippers. The animal then was stretched out and maneuvered into position for sacking.

Upon conclusion of my IGY activities we had crated the following: four Galápagos penguins, seven land iguanas, five sea iguanas, two tortoises and three Galápagos sea lions. It was wonderful news when I learned that the tuna clipper *Mary Barbara* was headed for San Cristobal to take me aboard.

Fred Kunzel, president of the Zoological Society, had conferred with the administrator of National Marine Terminal to see if any of their tuna clippers were operating near the Galápagos. The *Mary Barbara* had passed the islands and already was nearing Costa Rica, with its crew anxious to return home. But a radio message from headquarters in San Diego prompted the ship to retrace its course.

Crew members willingly helped to keep our little menagerie alive. And in twelve short days we arrived in San Diego—home at last!

Edna Henblein

# Counting Elephants at Kilaguni

## By Edna Heublein

*Editors tend to experience life vicariously through the eyes of the writers whose stories they print. Now and then, however, they are allowed a glimpse of the real thing. Edna Heublein, who served 20 years as ZOONOOZ editor, describes one such glimpse.*

**September 1978**

It is 6:45 in the evening—the sun is setting behind the cloudbank that shrouds the twin peaks of Kilimanjaro. Out of the scattered acacias looms a large gray form—it is the leader of the elephant herd making a resolute line toward the waterholes. The old cow goes to the far hole to drink; two other adults circle the largest pool and also start to drink. Then several juveniles test the edges of the pool. Altogether, there are seven adults and five youngsters; the smallest easily walks under its mother.

Floodlights come on to the left. Egyptian geese swim around quietly in one of the pools... a marabou stork somberly sits in a treetop... overhead hundreds of swifts offer their sharp, shrill twittering calls as they catch the insects attracted by the lights. The entire side of Kilaguni Lodge which faces the waterholes is open, permitting the birds to go in and out at will. The swifts attach their nests to the beams of the lodge ceiling.

By this time, it is 7:15 and two stars are twinkling over the elephants that are moving from the largest pool to a smaller one which looks like only a puddle, but all the animals still fit in. Then the newest baby and its mother lead the parade to a third pond. After bathing, each baby elephant rubs its body against its mother's legs. Some of the larger elephants are leaving... but others emerge from the darkness and walk toward the waterholes.

Dinner for lodge guests is announced with a roll of drums... the elephants stop all activity... then an animal's shriek breaks the night, and the elephants lift their trunks for a moment, but resume drinking almost immediately. One of the mothers dusts herself with the red earth... others follow suit.

*Elephant herd at Kilaguni, with Mount Kilimanjaro in the background.*

Two buffalos come to drink... several elephants prepare to leave and the tiny baby scrambles up the bank in order to go along with its mother. Another baby entertains itself by chasing some cattle egrets. A Black-necked Heron flies across the clearing—and a new group of elephants is coming to drink. By this time we have counted 41 elephants—females with babies and juveniles; two females each with two young, one baby and a juvenile. After a while we saw two males standing close to each other for a long time, then another male appeared, and another, until there were nine... the boys appeared to be having a meeting at the pond. By 9:45 two bulls had disappeared as silently as they had come... several rubbed on a large rock—they first rubbed each side and then the hind quarters. Our count of elephants had reached 123... and small groups of 6, 7, and 8 were still coming and going.

By midnight, all the other guests had retired. Reluctantly, I also gave up watching from that comfortable chair on the veranda and hurried to my room, for I remembered that it had a balcony. From there, I now saw only one large elephant standing as sentinel at the left side of the pools... he turned toward me the moment I stepped outside, that lone elephant of Tsavo.

A half hour or so later, before going to sleep, I went out on the balcony for a second viewing. To my surprise, the waterholes were alive again with little groups of animals, mostly elephants—they would drink, bathe, then just stand—and finally move off into the shadows, swallowed up by the night. Occasionally, a snort, perhaps a disagreement, or maybe just a greeting broke the absolute quiet with which these animals carried on their activities. They moved like phantoms, not even a twig cracked underfoot.

It was difficult to go to bed—but in the morning would be another game run, very early...

# Beginner's Africa

## By Kenhelm W. Stott, Jr.

*Ken Stott, who has served the Zoo in too many categories to list, here describes in a manner reminiscent of Mark Twain's* Innocents Abroad, *the first leg of his long ago and long-anticipated foray into the Dark Continent.*

**January 1950**

The Mediterranean, bluer than ever postcards would presume to admit, was speckled with billowing, triangular sails of fishing craft, bobbing their way toward Crete, which rose from the low mists ahead. Beautiful as the scene was, I let it slip past almost unnoticed, certainly unappreciated.

For twenty years I had dreamt the dream of many naturalists, that of seeing the big game continent; of discovering that the Africa of Carl Akeley, of Edmund Heller, of Martin and Osa Johnson existed not merely on the printed page but actually in terms of soil, air, and water.

Almost without realizing what was happening, I watched a thin line of breakers pass beneath the plane. The steward touched my arm and pointed through the window. As he did so, he whispered a single, electrifying word.

"Alexandria!"

Here was Africa at last! The mass of dimly outlined cubes and rectangles below us might just as easily have been Palm Springs or Barstow, but they were not. This was Africa—scarcely the acacia and grassland Africa of the Johnsons nor the humid, bejungled Africa of Stanley, but honest-to-goodness Africa, nonetheless.

As we gradually lost altitude, the scene took on detail. Slow-moving camel caravans moved across the sands toward curious, jumbled mud villages which rose from the rich soil of the delta, and native boats under full sail crept up the river. Ahead Cairo's minarets and opalescent domes came into sight.

The terminal, a bleak, sprawling two-story building, seemed admirably suited to its surroundings. Once inside, I fell in at the end of a sweating line and apprehensively prepared to submit my credentials.

A dapper official in a Palm Beach suit, a red fez, and a monocle took my customs declaration and began to check over the contents of the baggage. Suddenly he stopped and accusingly announced, "You have a camera!'

I could see no reason to deny it since he was holding the camera in his hand, so I pointed out that I also had a dozen rolls of film, a telephoto lens, a pair of binoculars, and various other equipment which is fairly standard with naturalists.

"Don't you know that Egypt is at war?" he asked.

I assured him that I was quite aware of the fact but surely, even in wartime, such equipment could be taken through the country sealed in bond. He looked at me as though he had never heard of the procedure. Then he put the camera down, disappeared for a moment, and returned with a fistful of forms and regulations.

"Read these, and fill out the others. Then we will seal your equipment." He indicated a desk in the far corner of the room. "Don't worry about your luggage, it will be quite safe here."

Eventually, I completed them and slipped back to the customs bench and my luggage. I looked for the official with whom I had spoken before but he was nowhere to be seen. Then I looked down at my luggage. All of my photographic equipment was gone!

As calmly as possible I asked one of the attendants where "my" official had gone. "Which official?" he wanted to know.

"The one with the monocle." Seeing no gleam of recognition in the man's eyes, I went on to describe the official in greater detail.

The attendant looked at me with wide, bewildered eyes. "There is no one here of that description." Then he smiled comfortingly and said, "Don't worry. He was probably an imposter."

With that, I lost the last semblance of composure and began shouting at the top of my lungs. He bowed stiffly, backed off, and called the other attendants into a huddle. Although he spoke in Arabic, it was obvious he was describing the "official" carefully. He stroked an imaginary goatee, patted a non-existent red fez, and peered through a thumb-and-forefinger monocle.

When he finished, the group turned to me as a body. In unison they shrugged their shoulders and shook their heads.

Somehow, I managed to thank them. I hastily strapped up and locked my luggage and set about searching the building.

I attracted an interested and rather sympathetic group of followers who pattered along behind me, helpfully peering under crates and into piles of rubbish which had accumulated in the corners.

After half an hour of frantic and disorganized search throughout both floors of the building, I began throwing open office doors in sheer desperation. The occupants took little notice of my actions—apparently such was of common occurrence. Finally, in a dingy and rather inconspicuous little alcove, I pulled a door open and there sitting behind a desk was my official with his hands folded and a benign expression on his face. On the desk in front of him lay my equipment.

In soft reproach, he explained, "We never conduct this sort of business in the main hall. It always must be done in my office!"

Fortunately, I was by this time quite speechless. I handed him the forms, which he looked over briefly.

"Now, if I may have twenty Egyptian pounds for the duty fee, I will fill out a receipt and give you your equipment. You will be refunded the money when you leave Egypt or the Sudan providing you do not break the seal."

I asked him if he would accept a traveler's check in dollars.

*Kenya: the Africa of Martin & Osa Johnson.*

"I'm very sorry. We can only accept Egyptian pounds."

I asked him where at the airport I could get a check cashed. He regretted that there was no place where I might cash one except in town.

"You mean I've got to go into town, cash a check, then come back?'

He threw up his hands in horror. "Oh, you can't come back! You can't come back into the terminal unless you are leaving on a plane–and as I understand it, you are going up the river by train and boat into the Sudan."

How could I get the camera if I would not be permitted to return to the field? He was extremely sorry but he did not know. He hastened to assure me, however, that the equipment would be kept locked in his safe.

There was nothing more I could do there so I stomped out of the office, collected the rest of my luggage, and carried it to the waiting bus outside. Once I had entered, the bus lurched into action and I found myself sitting in the lap of a very large and very surprised Egyptian lady. I rose, searched for some shred of remaining dignity and moved to another, less luxuriantly upholstered seat.

As I watched the blazing dunes bounce by, I ground my teeth. So this was Africa!

# Dread Danakil

## By Kenhelm W. Stott, Jr.

*Nearly twenty-five years and many safaris later (but in the same wryly humorous manner), Stott takes us along on a hazardous foray into Ethiopia's forbidding Danakil Depression. Stott, in addition to his many other honors, is a fellow of the prestigious Explorers' Club.*

**February 1974**

Danakil—jagged ranges of black lava-strewn hills jutting up from sunscorched plains of ochre stubble, or vast flat sheets of blinding white salt and sand; an occasional lake, reed-lined with a peripheral band of silvery tamarisk scrub.

At the upper and southern end of the 400-mile-long valley flows the muddy Awash bordered by branching doum palms and acacia thornbush. Beginning and ending in eastern Ethiopia, the river gradually dissipates, some of its waters reaching minor landlocked lakes to the east, the remainder soaked hungrily by parched desert soil or evaporating into zero-humidity atmosphere.

Rainfall varies from ten inches per annum in some restricted areas to a stark nil in others. At the northern end of the valley lies the Danakil Depression, nearly 400 feet below sea level. Hardly spectacular, the Danakil is nonetheless awesome.

Understandably, density of human population is low. It consists primarily of semi-nomadic Danakils, lightly clothed but heavily laden with shields, spears, pangas and rifles. Tall, dark, sinuously muscular, the Danakils are as fierce as they look. They guard enormous herds of undernourished dromedaries, donkeys, cattle and goats assiduously and are not in the least averse to stock rustling, an activity that promotes continuous tribal warfare.

Other human beings who live or must pass through the area are fair game to the Danakils with the result that the human remains one encounters are quite democratically those of all available races, colors and creeds. Vultures and an over-abundance of hyenas, both spotted and striped, flourish.

Our own involvement with the Danakil Valley began in Nairobi. There we contacted Roger McKay, who has a reputation for leading safaris into areas more conservative competitors are reluctant to invade.

Our plan was simple: Roger and staff were to drive two vehicles to Addis Ababa while Jack Selsor, a San Diego Zoological Society

*Soemmerring's gazelle.*

patron, and I arrived by air. By this time he had enlisted the aid of Gray Goodman, a young American wildlife buff who had grown up in Ethiopia, and Urs Carol, a Swiss commercial bush pilot. As Gray spoke English and Amharic, verbal communication with the Danakils was now possible, a convenience which would not only prove invaluable but subsequently may well have saved our lives.

Gray, Jack and I left Addis during a torrential downpour, wending our way past overturned trucks, headon collisions, and the other hazards that are promoted by narrow mountain roads, extreme weather conditions, and poorly maintained mechanical equipment.

Gradually, we left the chill and damp of the highlands behind, passed through shadowy agricultural lands into lowland bush.

Ahead, a scattering of soft, flickering lights marked the location of Awash where we were to spend the night. It was now 2 a.m. Accommodations consisted of a somewhat grubby room, sans facilities but with clean linen and the reassuring presence of an armed guard outside the door. Later, we were awakened by the shattering arrival of Roger McKay's battered Land Cruiser, filled to capacity with staff, tents, lamps, stoves, food and medical supplies, and drums of airplane fuel.

Beyond Awash, the tarmac came to an end. We left the main road and followed a hazardous 25-kilometer track, alternately studded with jagged rocks or plunging into mounds of powder-fine silt. One extreme involved lifting (by hand or jack) our vehicles over the high stones, or extracting the cars from sandbeds—with time out for a tire change or two. At 115° F, tire-changing is anything but pleasurable.

Fifteen kilometers further on we reached a cliff overlooking Lake Hertale. There, we established base camp. Below us, Nile crocodiles, some of impressive size, and hippopotami

(one group of at least 70 individuals) wallowed in murky waters and dispelled any thoughts we had entertained of a refreshing swim.

Less timid neighbors proved to be Danakils in full regalia and well armed. Their welcome was something less than enthusiastic—as they sheathed and unsheathed their pangas, testing razor-sharp edges for effect. We were made to understand that it would be well to hire three or four of the fifteen warriors in attendance as "guards." Since there was nothing in the vicinity to be guarded from but the Danakils themselves, we promptly hired four of their number, the chief included. All fifteen then squatted in the shade of the tent flap, scratched because of assorted ectoparasites, rattled their varied armament, and grinned non-benevolently. During the nights that followed, Jack and I were never convinced that our trusty guards might not slash the tents, remove our valuables, and last but not least us.

First priority consisted of clearing an abandoned dirt airstrip of brush, stones and pigholes. Next, camp equipment had to be put into semi-functioning order: butane lamps, evaporation-type waterbags, petrol tins filled with boiled water, kerosene fridge fueled, started and stocked. Guaranteed to keep meats frozen at an external temperature of 110°F, it proved no match for Danakil heat. Ultimately crocodiles ate more than we did of the lamb, beef, and pork so carefully transported from Nairobi.

The relative coolness of morning and afternoon was reserved for game runs. Reedbeds and tamarisk stands bordering the lake provided haven for abundant wildlife.

Early one morning, Jack and I awoke to the distant drone of an aircraft. Within minutes, a gleaming white and red Comanche buzzed our camp. Shortly, Urs Carol, also in gleaming white and red, appeared. A handsome dark-haired fellow in his early thirties, Urs was invariably impeccable while the rest of us were grubby from dawn to dusk, safe water being in short supply and murky enough to render clothing a bit grimier with each washing. Urs somehow managed two or three complete clothing changes per day. But he was without exception the best bush pilot we have yet to encounter.

After refueling the Comanche, we took off from Hertale, leaving our "guarded" camp behind. Roger and Gray were to follow by surface, the Land Cruiser heavily loaded with fuel drums. Our goal was the construction camp at Km. 270.

We had never seen a landscape of such utter and colorless desolation. Vegetation seemed non-existent. Yet here and there, herds of Soemmering's gazelle and oryx loped across the flatlands, Abyssinian ground hornbills and

Danakil Valley

Awash National Park

Addis Ababa
Area 1
Area 2
Km. 270
Depression
Awash
Lake Hertale
Km.112
Assab
N

RED SEA
Massawa
Eritrea
Assab
GULF OF ADEN
Danakil Valley
French Territory
White Nile
Blue Nile
Blue Nile Gorge
Addis Ababa
Awash
Awash National Park
Awash River
ETHIOPIA
SUDAN
SOMALI REPUBLIC
INDIAN OCEAN
KENYA
N

*Kenhelm W. Stott, Jr.*

kori and Arabian bustards strutted militantly, and North African ostriches raised their heads to scan the sky for our plane. Grevy's zebras, singly or in pairs, picked their way up rocky slopes.

Km. 270 offered no landing strip, so Urs slipped smoothly onto the uneven surface of a half-completed roadway. A waiting Land Rover bounced us away to an air-conditioned trailer where Trapp Company employees served cold drinks and luncheon.

The Somali wild ass, (*Equus asinus somalicus*) headed the list of creatures we most wanted to find in the Danakil. It was, in fact, the primary reason for the excursion. Probably never abundant, its range currently extended from the Danakil Depression south into Somalia. In Ethiopia it occurs only between the Depression and Lake Hertale. It is doubtful if the total population exceeds a few hundred. Larger than the Nubian Ass, (*E. a. asinus*) from which the common domestic donkey descends, the Somali form is pale, almost pearl gray above and white below.

After lunch, the three of us took off again. On this flight we headed east, climbing first over a drear dessicated plateau, then on into an equally arid valley, and dashing through a narrow gorge in a range of 1,500-foot volcanic hills.

Some twenty miles from camp we emerged onto a broad, barren salt plain. Suddenly, Urs pointed triumphantly towards a spot dead ahead where the black of the lava hills gave way to the white of the pan. Three gray forms marched single-file along a well-worn trail at the base of the hills.

We swooped downward to a 30-foot level and the trio of Somali Wild Ass broke into a gallop, moving out onto the pan. Urs circled the plain, selected what appeared to be a stoneless level stretch and landed, our wheels crunching as they broke through the crisp surface of the salt bed. After pulling to a stop, Urs handed us one rifle with two shots and pointed out the only two bushes on the entire pan. He instructed each of us to hide behind one of the scraggly shrubs. The rifle was to serve in case hostile Danakils put in an appearance. I left the rifle with Jack since, should the need to use the weapon arise, he stood less chance of shooting off his own foot than I.

My shrub lay about an eighth of a mile away. I have no idea what the temperature was but I have never been warmer at any time, in any place. Dark glasses reduced the painful glare only slightly and instant evaporation kept the sweatband of my brimmed hat bone-dry. Mountains surrounding the pan rippled through the heat waves and distant nonexistent lakes shimmered tantalizingly. Fiery blasts of wind whipped clouds of dust into the air. By this time, Urs had taken off again and Jack and I had taken up our positions under our respective bushes which unfortunately offered little shade.

Urs slowly circled the plain, the objective being to gently drive the asses between our two outlooks. But this was not to be. The fact

*Hippos on the shores of Lake Hertale.*

that Somali wild asses survive at all is due to an uncanny wariness and keen eyesight. Despite the fact that we were lying flat and motionless on the scorched ground beneath our scruffy bushes, the asses sauntered across the plain making a broad circle around us.

Flying back to camp, we passed over other wild asses, some on the flat lands, others climbing rocky cliffs with mountain-goat agility, and on subsequent flights we saw additional wild asses—sometimes singly or in pairs, or small parties up to five.

Eventually, our supply of aviation fuel ran low, so there was no choice but to return to base camp.

In our absence, our Danakil guards had come to the conclusion that they were being underpaid. They made it clear (a throat-slashing gesture is the same in any language) that we would either up the ante or they would kill us, a prospect that seemed temptingly appealing (to them). We needed little prompting to meet their additional demands: the gigantic sum of four Ethiopian dollars, equivalent to two United States dollars. Little did they know that, if pressed further, we might even have doubled the amount.

We look back upon our Danakil adventure with mixed emotions. Its grotesque though hardly attractive terrain, its vegetation or lack of same, its remarkable fauna, and most certainly the Danakil tribesmen themselves—all were unique. However, we would most assuredly not care to live there; in fact, we doubt that it could even be considered that proverbial "nice place to visit."

# A Visit to Heron Island

## By Kenton C. Lint

*Kenton C. Lint retired in 1976 after 40 years at the Zoo, 28 of them as curator of birds. K.C., an active curator emeritus, continues to be recognized as one of the world's leading authorities on avian subjects. This 1977 article shows him at his knowledgeable best.*

**January 1977**

Geologists believe that Australia has been isolated by sea from other land masses for sixty million years. Thus protected, the primitive marsupials, such as the koalas, the kangaroos and wallabies, the possums, and most primitive of all, the egg-laying platypus, were able to survive long after many of their counterparts in other continents had been eliminated by higher forms of life. In this isolation, there developed also some of the world's most beautiful and curious birds.

Heron Island is situated on the Great Barrier Reef, 45 miles off the Queensland coast. Heron is a true coral islet, a haven for 45 species of sea and land birds, for the unwieldy sea turtles which struggle ashore to lay their eggs from late October to April, and for 1,500 varieties of brightly hued fish which dart among the fantastic growth of sun-seeking coral. A Marine National Park, this 42-acre coral island is covered with native foliage. It is ringed with white sandy beaches and surrounded by 12 square miles of colorful coral reef.

Sea birds breed on land, but they are bound to the sea for their food. Heron Island has a large population of these sea birds, both resident and periodic. In addition, there are land birds associated solely with the island and others that are accidental visitors from the mainland.

Heron Island was named after the Reef heron. This large bird can be observed at low tide out on the reef flat stalking its prey. It has a long pointed bill, long yellowish-green legs and feet, and a short tail. It builds a nest of sticks and small branches high in the trees toward the interior of the island.

Reef herons congregate in the trees that grow on the perimeter of the island while waiting for the tide to drop sufficiently to enable them to forage on the reef. There they seek the small crustaceans, fish and mollusks that comprise their diet.

Probably the most conspicuous bird on Heron Island is the white-capped noddy tern, with an estimated population of 17,000. It

K.C. Lint

breeds and remains on this island throughout the year, except to seek food. Both adults and fledged young leave the island early in the morning. The young birds return in the afternoon, but the adults do not come back until just before dark when they feed the young. White-capped noddy terns fish by skimming the surface water where they capture the 3-inch-long hardy heads that frequent the Capricorn and Bunker groups.

It roosts and nests primarily in the pisonia trees, which grow 20 to 50 feet in height. The seed pods are covered with a sweet gum which attracts birds, hence its common name, bird-catcher tree. The tern population on Heron Island is regulated by storms which may kill or injure large numbers annually.

The black-naped tern is unable to compete with man on Heron Island. It has formed a small colony on the wreck of the ship *Sydney* that acts as a breakwater at the harbor entrance. Nesting of this fork-tailed tern takes place on the rusting ship each year in summer.

The silver gull meets all visitors arriving at the helicopter pad adjacent to the harbor. it is almost entirely white, with a pale gray back and black tips to the wings. The red ring around the white eye matches the legs and feet. The range of this beautiful gull extends around the whole coastline of Australia. It also travels to offshore islands, and in flood years it may fly as far inland as Lake Eyre.

The wedge-tailed shearwater inhabits Heron Island from October to May. A medium-sized member of the petrel group, it is not a migratory bird in the true sense, but disperses from the breeding grounds after nesting, possibly as far as New Guinea. The shearwater nests by burrowing into the ground. The nesting tunnel may be 3 meters in length, ending in a chamber lined with grass where the single egg is incubated by both adults. The chick is fed at night by both parents and left unattended during the day.

The courting of the shearwater prior to egg-laying occurs at night, with an eerie wailing that terminates in shrill cries. The vocalizations reminded me of the wailing of domestic tom cats.

The adults forsake the nest before the chicks are fully fledged. Thus the young live for a time on the accumulation of reserve fat. They must also learn to fly on their own. As soon as their wings are full grown and strong enough, they fly out to sea to join their parents as open-sea birds.

Because of its extensive wingspread and limited take-off area, the shearwater runs along well-defined paths toward openings in the vegetation, taking off near the shore. On returning after dark, it lands near the burrow, pancake fashion. While extremely clumsy on the ground, the wedge-tailed shearwater is a delight to watch in the air, as it glides

Phillip T. Robinson

effortlessly inches above the water, feeding on great schools of small fish and crustaceans.

Heron Island is the only national park and refuge in the world where one may share a sandwich with the banded landrail, one of several land birds common to that island. This small rail performs a valuable service by controlling the grub and insect population. However, it is becoming adapted to human association, where much of the food is provided by man. Consequently, this large banded and spotted brown rail wins friends quickly. Usually it is a secretive bird, and while flight is possible, the lack of predators on the island makes it favor walking.

*Heron Island native: The white-capped noddy tern.*

# Sketchbook of East Africa

## By Charles Faust

*Much of what you see at the San Diego Zoo and Wild Animal Park springs from the genius of Charles Faust, our longtime designer. His 1969 visit to East Africa provided the inspiration for the architecture and ambiance which distinguish the Wild Animal Park.*

**February 1970**

"Only by an actual visit can one feel the fascination and see the beauty that is Africa." Each time similar sentiments were expressed to me, my response was a bit more skeptical, probably the result of a surfeit of color slides and travel films.

Then in September, 1969, Mrs. Faust and I joined the San Diego Zoological Society's Safari to East Africa; and my skepticism vanished as I worked to capture the beauty. Most of the smaller sketches were done enroute and sometimes with my pad held in midair due to the rugged road conditions. The larger drawings and water colors were started in the evenings and finished whenever time permitted.

The tour group flew from Los Angeles to London, and then to Uganda. The lush, tropical Uganda countryside, the beauty of Queen Elizabeth National Park, the crossing of the equator twice, and the enchanting morning on the Kazinga Channel left lasting impressions.

The next day's landscape was entirely different—our route took us close to the hazy Ruwenzori Mountains along the Congo border, a land pock-marked with giant craters of extinct volcanoes, but beautifully covered with quilts of brilliant green and yellowing game grass and throbbing and pulsating with all kinds of animal life.

The following day, we wound our way across the Bunyoro district, reaching Murchison Falls National Park in time for an afternoon view of the rainbow-shrouded, thundering

*Hippos on the banks of the Nile.*

At the Masai village on the floor of the Ngorongoro Crater one must make arrangements for close examination of the village and for photographs with the village chief. He is standing at the right with spear and shield. The cattle compound is in the center surrounded by about a dozen family huts. Walls are constructed by plastering a mixture of manure and earth over branches bent in an arc and stuck into the ground; other branches are woven horizontally. A single doorway into each hut is on the outside of the circle. To keep out prowling animals at night, the head of the family pulls a stick-and-thorn woven mesh door across the entrance.

C.R. Faust

torrent. In the lower stretches, the river calms down to form the Victoria Nile which was crossed by pontoon ferry to reach Paraa Lodge, perched high on the far bank.

We cruised to the foot of the falls in a motor launch, an annoyance to the suspicious African buffalo grazing along the banks and the hundreds of crocodiles, birds, elephants and hippos inhabiting the region.

The Pakuba area, visited in the afternoon, had hartebeest, oribi, and Uganda kob bounding about in the savanna's tall grasses. Among the trees along the banks of the Albert Nile, the stately maneuvers of numerous giraffe and the lumbering tactics of buffalo and rhino could be seen.

The return leg took us eastward to Nakasongola and through the Mengo district to Entebbe. This wind-up gave us things to mull over during our flight across Lake Victoria into Nairobi, Kenya's colorful, bustling capital.

After crossing the Athi Plains and the district of the Masai, all flat, arid country, we arrived at the Lake Manyara National Park where game is more concentrated than in any other area, even including tree-climbing lions. Then on to Ngorongoro for a two-night stay at the game lodge on the rim of the crater.

Saturday was spent in game viewing in Landrovers down on the crater floor—there were large herds of wildebeest, zebra, lion, buffalo and many other plains game. We visited a Masai village which proved so fascinating as to result in a full color painting.

*Secretary birds in a high bush nest.*

Tourists
photograph
Thomson's
gazelle in
Uganda game
reserve.

Warthogs trot
over the East
African plains.

Seronera Lodge probably offered the most outstanding native hut construction we were to see—very high-pitched thatched roofs were perched atop the rounded structures. The afternoon drive took us to Serengeti National Park, noted for its large migratory concentration of plains game. There thousands of animals live together in a delicately balanced relationship with one another.

Our last game viewing experience was done from 40 feet above the ground at the lookout hotel known as "Treetops." After the party is installed in the hotel, the entrances are locked and no one can leave until morning. The main attraction that brings animals to this site is a natural water hole and cobalt deposits in the soil along with a man-made salt lick. The entire roof is a viewing platform and one can go up there to survey the countryside.

*Thatched native huts, Uganda (above) and sleeping huts on the Serengeti plains, designs Faust incorporated into the Wild Animal Park.*

(preceding page) American bald eagle (Haliaeetus leucocephalus). Photo by R. Van Nostrand.

(upper left) Ostrich (Struthio camelus). Photo by David Detchmendy.

(upper right) Great egret (Egretta alba). Photo by R. & Mary Van Nostrand.

(below) Yellow-throated sandgrouse (Pterocles gutturalis)

*(upper left) Kea (Nestor notabilis)*

*(upper right) Count Raggi's bird of paradise (Paradisaea raggiana)*

*(below) Schalow's touraco (Tauraco corythaix schalowi). Photo by R. Van Nostrand*

*(above) Magpie goose (Anseranas semipalmata)*

*(below) King bird of paradise (Cincinnurus regius)*

# A Grand Old Bird

## By Maureen L. Greeley

*King Tut and ZOONOOZ are virtually the same age and for over half the three score years he has been in residence, Tut has been the Zoo's official greeter, welcoming visitors from his perch in the Dryer Flamingo Lagoon. As he celebrates his 60th anniversary on the throne, we join with all his followers in saying, "Long live the king!"*

**February 1985**

His bearing is that of a king—a king who has reigned long and reigned well—a king who is well loved. His royal crown of salmon hues and his cloak of brilliant white add to his stately appearance, and he wears his years of experience with grace. His has been a long and interesting life.

King Tut, a salmon-crested cockatoo, was obtained in Singapore in 1925 by the famed animal collector Frank (Bring-'em-Back-Alive) Buck. Tut was already an adult bird when he arrived in San Diego 60 years ago, on March 25, 1925.

During those early years, Tut's time was divided between the I.D. Putnam aviaries, the Zoo, and various motion picture and theatrical duties, including work with the fan dancer Sally Rand.

On February 19, 1951, King Tut returned to the Zoo to take up his permanent position as Official Zoo Greeter. He did not retire from show business at that time. Appearances on the long-running "Zoorama" television program, produced by KFMB-TV in cooperation with the Zoo, and in productions at the Old Globe Theatre and the Starlight Opera Company in San Diego kept him busy.

It is at the Zoo, however, that King Tut truly reigns supreme. From his perch in the Dryer Flamingo Lagoon he is a proud ruler, entertaining his public and demanding their attention. His antics have, perhaps, slowed a bit in recent years, but Tut still whistles, sings, and dances his greetings on occasion.

There have been other reports of cockatoos living as long as 60 years; reports of more than 75 years are questionable. Sixty years for a cockatoo are equivalent to more than a hundred years for a human being.

Cockatoos are popular for their intelligence and their mimicking abilities. Tut can say a few words, whistle a few songs, cry like a baby, meow like a cat, cluck like a chicken, and emit an ear-piercing squawk when it's attention he's after.

It is Tut's tame, affectionate, and gentle disposition that make him a most beloved ruler. We salute him on his 60th anniversary and hope that he will reign for many years more.

# Painting . . .
# Elephant Style

## By Joan Embery

*Can an elephant paint? Carol does! Her canvases have been hailed as excellent examples of impressionism—and she works for peanuts. Joan Embery, who taught the pachyderm to paint, is the Zoo's goodwill ambassador and is well-known to American audiences through her many television appearances.*

### October 1970

I first became interested in Carol Elephant while working as an attendant in the Children's Zoo. I found her to be very sociable, agile and inteligent, and highly responsive to attention. But like most elephants, she has a mind of her own and quickly learns to take the upper hand whenever possible.

A trainer must assert his authority at the first sign of rebellion to prevent the sly tricks of squeezing, pushing and slapping that many elephants use to haze a keeper. Since I had no experience in training elephants, we learned together.

I learned how to use the bull hook, a stick with a blunt hook on the tip. The hook does not hurt the animal. It learns to move away from the hook when pressure is applied to it, accompanied by a vocal command. Eventually all that is necessary is the vocal command. When the elephant obeys, she is rewarded with a piece of fruit or vegetable.

Carol's true fame came when she gained national recognition as an artist. Several of her paintings have sold for $100 each, and we have had inquiries about her work from around the country. The money from the sales of her paintings has gone into a special animal acquisition fund for the San Diego Wild Animal Park.

*Trainer Joan Embery furnishes a little artistic criticism.*

*An elephant's effort with paint can be appreciated from any angle. The footprint (lower left) and the trunk mark (upper right) serve as Carol's signature.*

# Kakowet

## By Sheldon Campbell

*On an early African safari, Dr. George Pournelle, then curator of mammals, acquired a young bonobo, or pygmy chimpanzee. For the next 20 years, Kakowet was the pet personality of visitors and Zoo employees alike. Sheldon Campbell, a longtime Kakowet watcher, took this fond look back at his life and accomplishments.*

**December 1980**

Stories about Kawowet abound, created faster than he, prodigious father, created babies with his soul mate, Linda.

Kakowet (an Africanized phonetic spelling of *cacaouette*, French for peanut) was, of all the animals ever kept in the San Diego Zoo, the closest to being human. Knowledgeable onlookers occasionally had the eerie feeling that he didn't belong in an exhibit, but should instead be going about work and play with the rest of us. The thought wasn't too farfetched. Pygmy chimps may well be the most closely related to humankind of all the great apes.

There are those who contend that Kakowet was a little more than human in displaying extraordinary intelligence and perception, mostly directed toward getting what he wanted in service, food, and sex. He learned quickly to recognize individually every Zoo employee with whom he came in contact, no matter how seldom. Attendants in the Children's Zoo, where Kakowet lived when he first came to San Diego, discovered to their delight that this gave them a great advantage over employees elsewhere in the Zoo. Whenever Kakowet spotted Dr. Charles R. Schroeder, then the Zoo director, off in the distance he went into his "Schroeder recognition routine"—a special dance with hoots. Because Dr. Schroeder was noted for surprise inspections, Kakowet provided an early warning system which enabled the Children's Zoo employees to look

*Kakowet researches the pygmy chimp's closest relative.*

HUMAN BEHAVIOR

their busiest when the boss came in.

Kakowet was born in the forest somewhere near the village of Inongo. When Kak arrived on June 17, 1960, he weighed about 15 pounds and was an estimated two years old.

Kakowet showed an early ability to outsmart his keepers. For a long period after he arrived, for example, attendants wondered whether he was retarded or incapacitated, for he appeared incapable of walking and as a consequence had to be carried from place to place. Then one day an attendant accidentally discovered that Kak was not only capable of walking, he regularly walked—unless, that is, an attendant were present to carry him.

Placed at last in the moated ape enclosure of the Children's Zoo, Kakowet soon devised an escape route. His subsequent escapes—and there were several—were apparently not motivated by any desire to achieve freedom. Kak left the exhibit to raid a nearby patch of Natal plums, for when he once tasted that fruit it became an overriding passion. As attendants closed in on him, he frantically stored plums in his mouth and under his armpits. When capture seemed imminent, he climbed back into the enclosure, generally shedding a few plums in the process, and proceeded to eat the fruit before it could be wrested from him. The aftermath was always the same—a bad case of hives, manifested by swollen eyes and large bumps all over his body.

One time, instead of seeking plums, he shuffled up the path to a walk-through pheasant cage and disappeared inside. Within the wink of an eye he emerged, walking hand-in-hand with a somewhat shaken visitor.

While Kakowet had many activities and interests, he enjoyed none more than sex. Even as a young ape he displayed sexual precociousness, an early sign perhaps of what turned out to be an astounding fact: when fully mature, he had a sperm count of one billion per cc compared to a normal human male's 80 to 120 million. His youthful displays of passion were sometimes amusing—as when he tried to make love to a teddy bear—and sometimes embarrassing, for he was totally uninhibited.

When Linda, two or three years Kakowet's senior, arrived here from Antwerp in 1962, the two soon formed a pair bond that remained firm—and touching to onlookers—up to the day Kak's heart gave out. Both he and Linda would languish if the other were not present. During a stay in the hospital—where it was found that he had an incurable kidney disease—Kakowet was so evidently lonely that Linda was taken to the hospital to keep him company. When they were together in their grotto, they spent many hours grooming, playing with their offspring (for they were excellent parents), or simply lying together with arms intertwined.

*Kakowet*

If Kakowet had been human, he would have deserved a conservation medal. He probably made a great contribution to the world by working to assure the future of an endangered species—the pygmy chimpanzee—threatened with extinction in its African habitat by the increasing encroachment of human beings. Few conservationists have enjoyed their work more than Kak. Someday, in fact, he may father a baby from beyond the grave, for six hours after Kakowet died, researchers recovered spermatozoa which are being kept viable in our 21st Century Ark, a frozen zoo where tissues are stored in liquid nitrogen for future use in conservation research.

# One Hundred and One Months in the Growth and Development of Mountain Gorillas

## By Belle J. Benchley

*Mbongo and Ngagi, two of the Zoo's most famous pre-war residents, were believed at the time (and for many years after) to be mountain gorillas, a highly endangered species. Some experts now believe that the pair were actually Grauer's gorillas, an equally rare sub-species of the lowland gorilla found in the mountains of eastern Zaire.*

**May 1940**

*Young Mbongo.*

On October the fifth, 1931, two young mountain gorillas arrived at San Diego. They had been captured nearly a year before by Martin Johnson and his wife, Osa, in the Alumbongo Mountains in the Kivu district of the Belgian Congo.

When they arrived they were probably between four and five years old with approximately six or seven months difference in their ages. They were jet black with long thick hair encircling their round faces like the hood of a baby's woolly flannel wrap. We weighed the crate, both with them in it and emptied, and found that their combined weight was two hundred and sixty-nine pounds.

At the time of their capture the natives reported to Martin Johnson that they were male and female. However, Johnson was not completely convinced and asked us to determine the sex of each.

It was not until the gorillas were in the Zoo for more than three years that we were able to determine beyond a doubt that both of them were males.

Gorillas have been reported as being not only fierce and mean, but moody, sulky creatures, with little interest in the affairs around them, and unwilling or unable to adapt themselves to circumstances and conditions of captivity. Our two gorillas entered into the life of our Zoo with less difficulty than any specimen that has come under my observance. They have had fewer fights than any two of the other great apes, regardless of sex.

It is true, however, that at first they showed complete indifference to the animals in adjoining cages and to the visitors who hung around the cages watching them. It was not until they had been in the Zoo many months that we perceived that this indifference was assumed, especially on the part of Ngagi. Mbongo very early began to show his crowd-consciousness by showing off for the benefit of visitors and openly responded to their applause. Within a day or two they obviously recognized their own keeper and from the first took the food he brought them and accepted his care as a matter of course.

Within the next few days they had displayed for us their whole galaxy of tricks, chasing, wrestling, chest beating. Their indifference toward the people who watched them seemed as though they were blind and deaf.

Their concern for each other and obvious mutual attachment was in great contrast to their indifference toward those of us who cared for them. Frequently they sat touching their hands or feet together in a way which was plainly not casual. If one seemed in trouble or ill the other exerted every effort to stimulate him to activity and to make some contribution to a better frame of mind. Even after eight years in a cage together, their love for each other is often shown by a gentle touch, or the laying of one great hand on the other's shoulder in a manner which is at once a gesture of affection and confidence.

Although gorillas have apparently a well deserved reputation of being difficult to keep alive and well in captivity, it now appears that they are not the delicate creatures they have been considered.

After years of observation we are thoroughly convinced that the greatest threat to their existence is the danger of contagion. In spite of the care we have taken to prevent contagion the gorillas have had severe colds twice. The two apes were completely quarantined so that the colds could not be spread throughout the anthropoid group. In spite of our care, however, they did spread like fire, and every one of the big fellows was soon seriously ill. The gorillas appeared to have no instinct for helping themselves but lay holding their hands toward us with a look of piteous appeal. Fortunately we were able to use vapor treatments to relieve their difficulties in breathing. Within a few days the serious affair was over.

In June, 1938, Mbongo suffered an injury to his right foot. The foot had been crushed, possibly by a sharp edge of a heavy log. We felt that rest and quiet would be the best treatment. Early in July sloughing of tissues between the toes, and along the outside of the foot indicated gangrenous condition of the foot. Finally we decided to use the squeeze cage; the foot was anesthetized and X-rayed. The entire wound was curetted; the third joints of the toes which had sloughed off were removed and the cavities packed with urea crystals. From that date the gorilla began to improve although all too slowly for our peace of mind.

Immediately following Mbongo's serious injury we decided that we must be prepared to separate the two gorillas, as Ngagi was becoming increasing dominant and showing signs of sexual maturity which might lead to fighting. The smaller gorilla seemed to glory in his security and actually taunted Ngagi through the fence. But to our surprise the larger gorilla seemed disconsolate at the loss of his cage mate; he suffered loss of appetite, refused to go into his house at night and, finally, to

*Mbongo in a favorite pose.*

comfort him, we moved Mbongo back into the adjoining sleeping room, where the big fellows could see and touch each other through the bars and sleep close together. Ngagi immediately moved his own bed of hay to the corner of the room nearest that opening.

Mbongo regained the weight he had lost rapidly and we could see no effect upon his buoyant nature from his injury and long seclusion.

So far as we can see their mental condition has remained very much what it was when they first arrived. They are very different from each other. Mbongo is much more buoyant and lighthearted and at the same time more easily depressed than Ngagi. We can easily imagine that Ngagi would now be the leader of his own band if he had remained in the wild. We doubt very much if Mbongo would ever have become a real leader. Mbongo is always ready to give up rather than argue his point but when actually forced to fight he is the fiercer and more clever fighter of the two.

There are very few people that Ngagi even tolerates, and he shows plainly his resentment of photographers, or too close observance, especially when he is eating. He frowns and glares at strangers. At times, when I am with him alone, he will frown and pull down his heavy brows, but at the same time his lips will twitch in his efforts to repress a pleasant look. Usually that means he wants a little coaxing or scolding and it is not unusual for him to turn around and lie down with his head close

*Ngagi (upper).*

*Mbongo (lower).*

to the bars and his big arms crossed on his breast after such a demonstration, indicating he would like to have me scratch his big symmetrical crest.

Neither of the gorillas shows any interest either in their own or each other's sex development. They have shown some interest in a female chimpanzee and her baby, and in the female gibbon at the time of her baby's birth, also. Yet even when such interest is evident there has never been anything of a sex display or activity unless the exaggerated strut and hunching of the massive shoulders as he strides about might be Ngagi's way of attracting the female in the next cage.

Their food remains fresh uncooked fruit and vegetables, with grains and seeds at times and from time to time a treat of stale crusty bread. They have a block of cattle salt which they consume by wetting their fingers, rubbing it on the salt and licking it off. They eat about thirty-five pounds of food a day. It consists of about ten pounds of citrus fruit, and a like amount of bananas, which they prefer quite green; the balance is divided between carrots, potatoes, celery, corn, lettuce, apples, watermelon and other seasonable fruit and vegetables. They have milk and eggs several times a week except in summer. They eat practically everything but the skin of their oranges and grapefruit. After eating the gorillas lean forward on their elbows and, using the hollow cup of their broad palms for a container, often bring the food they have just consumed up and masticate it over and over, like the chewing of the cud by the ungulates. Much of the time the food is brought up into their mouths without being completely expelled but at times they have even expelled it entirely upon a clean floor or shelf and eaten it again with great relish.

In one particular our gorilla history has been entirely different than any other captive gorilla. This is in complete absence of any attempt on our part to handle or train them. In every case any familiarity between them and the keeper or others has been the result of their own advances and desire. From time to time they establish some intimate connection between themselves and a rare person of their own choice which they permit with no one else. They dislike to adjust themselves to every new keeper and resent any changes in their habits and environment. We, therefore, try to have only one or two persons work about their cages or care for them.

The gorillas are naturally clean. They indulge, however, in scarcely any grooming of themselves or each other. As they become older there is less of the chest beating than formerly. But even in their maturity they hold the attention of the crowds of Zoo visitors that surround their cage longer than any other individual or species. There is undoubtedly a fascination about these creatures which I am at a loss to explain.

*Two years after the preceding article appeared in ZOONOOZ, Belle Benchley added this poignant postscript in noting the death of Mbongo, the mountain gorilla she had helped rear from infancy.*

### April 1942

Never has the death of any animal in the San Diego Zoo created so much personal feeling of sorrow or regret as that of Mbongo, the greatest gorilla that has ever been known to man. While Ngagi was the boss of the cage it was always Mbongo who took the lead in trying all things new and different, whether it was the pool, the tires, the trapezes or the solution of any problem. But during the ten and one half years the two great male gorillas occupied the comparatively small area of the cage they had done much to dispel the ugly rumors of vicious ferocity that had surrounded the gorilla and to give a clearer picture of the ape commonly thought of as the closest kin to man in the animal world.

*Ngagi.*

The autopsy revealed that Mbongo was still young; his bones were not as hard as would have been expected, nor was he sexually mature. Our estimate of Mbongo's age as nearing sixteen years, would indicate that the gorilla span of life might normally equal that of man.

The death of Mbongo occurred after a somewhat brief and baffling illness lasting a few days over three weeks. His temperature taken under considerable difficulty revealed nothing alarming; his respiration was not very rapid even on the day of his death. He ate no solid food but drank large quantities of milk or fruit juices by means of which the remedies, such as it is safe and possible to use with these great apes, could be administered. After death the cause was positively determined. It was due to the presence of the fungus, *Coccidioides immitis*, which had destroyed his lungs and had grown with a rapidity that in the three weeks had spread to several of his other organs. The disease, commonly called San Joaquin disease because of its frequency in the agricultural areas of that valley, is most prevalent among human beings, although infrequently cattle and some rodents are susceptible. This is the first time that the death of an ape has been thus accounted for. It is contracted from the earth or soil, possibly from heavy dust, as men have contracted the fungus when driving cattle, or more readily from clods of earth which harbor the spore.

The source of infection in this case might easily have been a small clod of earth, carrying the spore which had caught in the hay we used for bedding. Another possible source of infection could be from the clods which Zoo visitors pick up and toss at the gorillas to make them move about. In spite of keepers' constant watching, every Monday morning a big pan of rocks and clods are picked up which men and women have thrown into the cage. Their object is to hit an animal worth at least fifty thousand dollars, caring not if they put out an eye in their own desire to make him jump. Neither do they care if they give him a cold or any other disease which they might carry nor do they care if the clod might be the host of a deadly fungus.

# The Two-Headed Snake

## By Charles E. Shaw

*Perhaps few visitors would rank reptiles high on the list of their favorite creatures but one reptile at least was among the most popular Zoo exhibits ever. Charles E. Shaw, then curator of reptiles, reported on the arrival of Dudley Duplex, a two-headed kingsnake, in 1953.*

**January 1954**

In all probability two-headed snakes are not really the rarity they appear to be, for certainly only a very tiny number of those so born or hatched find their way to public notice. Always they are newly born or hatched specimens not more than a few weeks old. For the handicap posed by the possession by two heads of a single body is evidently tantamount to death at an early age. Both heads appear to be in an almost continual conflict of desires. The right head wants to move to the left, the left head to the right or vice versa. The net result of this antagonism,

or lack or cooperation, is that the rest of the body does not get much of anywhere until one head tires, the other gaining the upper hand and leading the way.

In Dudley Duplex the right head appears to be the dominant one. The heads are well separated, each being attached to the end of its own vertebral column which, from external appearances, evidently joins a common vertebral column about a half inch behind the rear of the heads. Anatomically, two-headed snakes may also show a rather bewildering assortment of internal organs. Sometimes there are two hearts and separate circulatory systems, one or two enlarged, functional lungs (snakes generally have only a single lung), two stomachs with but a single intestine, and various other peculiarities.

Mr. Duplex has perfectly formed heads joined at the throat by a webbing of normally scaled skin that somewhat restricts the freedom of movement of the individual heads. If, for example, the right head wishes to move to the right while the left head has made the decision to depart to the left, then this web of skin becomes stretched almost to the breaking point. In awkward instances such as this, the

*Dudley Duplex, the first of the Zoo's two-headed kingsnakes.*

forepart of the snake's body will rear off the floor of the cage, both heads straining to have their way and trembling mightily from the muscular effort.

In nature such snakes as this are at such a disadvantage in the struggle for existence that they seldom live more than a short time. One can easily imagine the difficulties two heads, each trying to control the body, would have in solving such problems as feeding, escape and even ordinary travel.

Feeding would undoubtedly pose the most serious handicap the snake would have to face. Insofar as catching living prey is concerned, it would seem almost impossible that there could be enough cooperation between the heads to accomplish this simple act of survival.

Captivity, of course, is a different matter altogether. Here the snake is protected from predators, and the food supply is adequate. Also the restricted freedom of the heads makes it less likely that they will become involved in arguments with one another. We need not fear for Dudley Duplex the fate that befell a two-headed individual in the Port Elizabeth Snake Park in South Africa. This double-headed specimen was endowed with relatively long necks which allowed considerable freedom of movement of the heads. The result was that one head devoured the other. The eatee, however, survived this harrowing experience. Some time later the eater was set upon with fratricidal intent by his neighbor with the unfortunate result that each bit the other until enough venom had taken effect to cause the death of the snake.

*A year later, Shaw filed this progress report on the snake with the split personality.*

We consider Dudley Duplex's longevity to be something of a triumph of matter over two minds. It cannot be said that he has been easy to live with. Feeding him has been the greatest trial and the most time-consuming part of his maintenance. Because of the possibility that one head may interfere with the other during feeding, Duplex has to be "sat with" through his meals. In the early days, such "snake sitting" sometimes took as much as an hour and a half. It is impossible to predict what thoughts will enter either head during the feeding process.

Take, for instance, the occasion of his feeding on February 5, 1954. Everything started out peacefully enough, and the expectation was that the right head, which is generally the dominant and more aggressive of the two, would, as usual, be the first to seize the proffered mouse. But the usually passive left head grabbed the mouse first. Right head immediately put a figurative foot down and grabbed the mouse by the rear. This sort of selfish attitude on the part of the right head was bound to get both heads precisely nowhere in the long run.

After much teasing, coaxing, threatening, and just plain cussing, right head was induced to part with his end of the meal so that left head could get on with it. Then, to placate right head, the aggressive member of this monstrous partnership was offered, via forceps, a succession of four mouse legs plus one juicy mouse rump. These anatomical tidbits he downed with pleasure and rapidity while left head patiently struggled with his whole small mouse. Being something of a novice concerning the basic mechanics of eating, he simply did not have the proper background of experience and training. This in spite of the fact that he dwelt only a head's length away, so to speak, from an accomplished gourmet.

At any rate, after running out of various and sundry mouse appurtenances with which to keep right head busy, it was somewhat discouraging to see him casually reach over and re-seize the mouse to which left head had earned sovereign right, at least by dint of effort. In attempting to separate the heads a second time, left head became excited and let go the mouse. The right head immediately grabbed it and finished it off in short order, while the unforunate left head was left to sulk in presumed frustrated rage.

Not always has the right head objected to the left head's desire to eat or has it always tried to hog it all. On March 12, right head was not even remotely interested in feeding,

*Dudley on the left, Duplex on the right.*

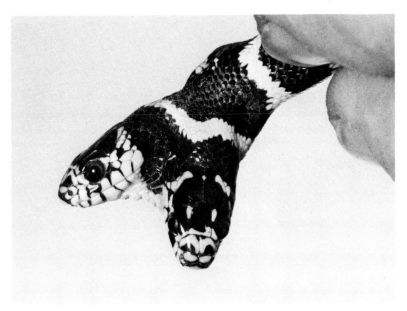

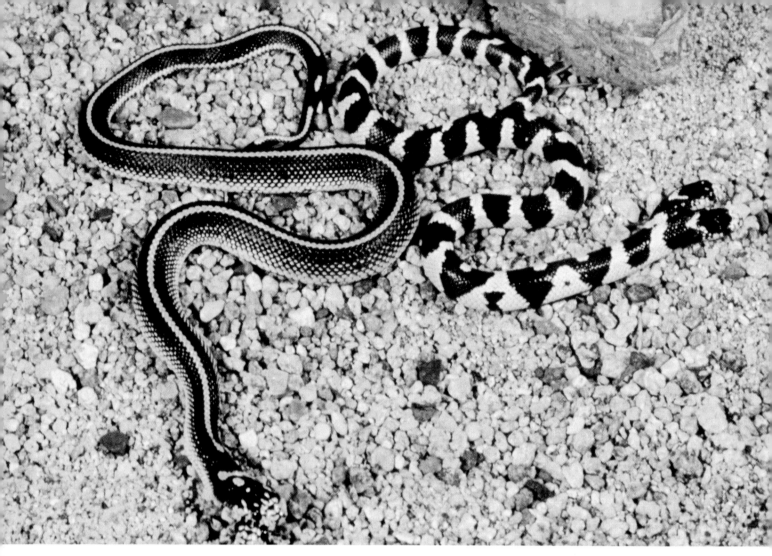

*Dudley Duplex with Nip-and-Tuck, another species of kingsnake, also two-headed.*

whereas left head seized the mouse immediately. However, right head simply would not stay still while the other head dined. Right head persisted in dragging the body all over the cage, so that in the end left head literally ate this meal on the run, and on mostly a backward run at that.

The most serious crisis in Duplex' life to date occurred when he was found to have snake mites, those almost microscopic parasitic spider-like creatures that can cause death. Our usual cure for this ailment is to soak the snake in water about as deep as the depth of the snake's body.

Duplex was removed from his cage and placed in a gallon jar in a shallow depth of water. But something went wrong with this previously infallible procedure, for the next day Duplex seemed all but dead. His heart was beating, but he appeared to be having some difficulty breathing.

Artificial respiration was administered off and on all day long, for whatever possible benefit it might have. Next morning, with great relief, it was noted that both heads were quite alert and that Duplex was crawling about the bottom of the gallon jar with both tongues flickering.

Skin shedding is generally difficult for Duplex because of the problem arising from the forking of his two short necks from the single body. In the only observed instance of this snake's shedding, it was, as might have been expected, the right head that initiated the proceedings, peeling its skin off to the juncture of the two necks.

At this point right head could go no farther since left head had done nothing about his own shedding and was content to let himself be dragged about the cage while right head was working furiously to get started on his end of the deal. Some four hours later, left head was observed to have gotten his own head skin off, but now both heads had stopped working at it, for the shedding process had been tied up at the fork-like juncture of the two independent necks.

Duplex was finally helped to the extent that the skin that had become caught was broken. Sometime later, right head recommenced the shedding process, removing the old skin back to the juncture of the two vertebral columns. From this point back, it was impossible to tell which head was controlling the body movements essential to proper shedding.

One of the few observed occasions in which the left head has taken the lead occurred while I was standing in front of the cage one afternoon. Left head suddenly opened his mouth in a very wide and lazy yawn. No sooner had left head closed his mouth than right head followed the leader. Perhaps, yawns are just as contagious in two-headed snakes as in humans.

*In November 1959, Dudley Duplex celebrated his/their sixth anniversary at the Zoo, making him/them the longest-surviving two-headed snake on record...and Shaw one of the greatest, if occasionally somewhat bemused, authorities on the subject.*

On November 6, 1953, there arrived at the San Diego Zoo a most exciting and unusual specimen, a two-headed California Kingsnake. Our ecstasy over this event was tempered by the realization that two-headed snakes were notoriously difficult to keep in capitivity. In fact, the longest any two-headed snake had survived in captivity was one year! We had quite a challenging as well as precious beast on our hands.

Unlike any ordinary snake with only a single operating end, Dudley Duplex, as he eventually became known, posed some delicate problems regarding feeding. Both heads had appetites and neither seemed to realize that no matter who did the eating, the tandem portion of the serpent would care for the nóurishment of the confused ''thinking''ends!

At first both heads usually became involved with the single mouse offered. Dudley, the right head, early showed himself to be the dominant and more aggressive member of this confusing partnership. For this reason, feeding appeared to become less of a problem with time. Dudley really seemed to ''learn'' how to eat more rapidly and efficiently than his ''slower'' neighbor, Duplex.

Though Duplex consistently maintained a desire to get in on the act, Dudley appeared to be able to down the mouse faster than Duplex could. To date, Dudley Duplex has eaten a total of 174 times; Duplex has dined alone only seven times, because of some reluctance of Dudley to participate in feeding at the time at all. Dudley and Duplex have supped together a total of 28 times; the remaining 139 feedings have been the exclusive gustatory pleasures of Dudley.

In spite of all the problems inherent in keeping this two-headed wonder, Dudley Duplex has far exceeded our prognostications as to his longevity. On November 6, Dudley Duplex celebrated his sixth anniversary with us. Dudley is about 31 1/2 inches long—somewhat under the average length of the ordinary, run-of-the-mill, single-headed kingsnake. This runted condition is probably the result of being the unfortunate prossessor of two very confused and confusing heads.

*By 1971, Dudley had been succeeded by Dudley Duplex II and Nip & Tuck. Though no longer the rarity it was 20 years earlier, the two-headed snake was still something the public found hard to believe.*

Possession and display of such a creature as a two-headed snake leads to considerable correspondence. Usually the letter writer has viewed the two-headed snake on a visit to the Zoo. Returning home, the viewer discusses the snake with friends or classmates—but no one believes the creature exists and its reality must be proven. A few examples:

"Last fall I visited your Zoo and while looking at your different snakes, I believe I saw a two-headed snake. During my college biology class, I mentioned the fact that I once saw a two-headed snake and I was immediately ridiculed by my classmates.

"Would you be so kind as to send me some verification of this snake, *if I saw it?*"

Another plea: "I, of course, was asked about the Zoo. I mentioned the two-headed kingsnake. Not knowing what a kingsnake was in the first place didn't help matters any.

"This letter is to ask for a little help in convincing some of these people that there is alive and living in the San Diegᴄ Zoo a two-headed snake."

From a lady in northern California: "Last evening I attended a cocktail party and I mentioned that I had seen your 'two-headed' snake, and that it was the only one of its kind in captivity. Of course, no one believed me! (Perhaps I was seeing double last night, but I know I was completely sober when I was at your Zoo.)

"I would appreciate either a letter or a post card verifying the fact that you do indeed have a 'two-headed' snake at the San Diego Zoo."

Another and obviously much younger correspondent had this to offer:

"I like your animals at your Zoo. I like the polar bears and tigers too. The monkeys are funny and so are gorillas too. I like the snake cause you have a two head king snake. You have big turtles. *Is there a two head snake?*"

It would appear that we have here another doubter of his own visual experience. Seeing doesn't necessarily lead to believing, especially if no one is willing to buy your tale of the two-headed snake at the San Diego Zoo.

# Albert the Great

## By Steven Joines

*Albert, a lowland gorilla, arrived at the Zoo in 1949 and for nearly 30 years ranked among its star attractions, a favorite with both the public and animal researchers. Steven Joines, one of the latter, reports on Albert's death in 1978.*

**February 1979**

Undoubtedly the most famous resident of the San Diego Zoo for the past three decades, the superb male lowland gorilla Albert died peacefully at 9:20 a.m. October 18, 1978 as a result of congestive heart failure. During the past year the effects of increasing age, heart trouble, and arthritis had caused him to slow down noticeably. He spent his last hours resting in his bedroom facility with his long-time keeper, Harold Mitchell, by his side.

On 15 August 1949 the San Diego Zoo became the first zoo in history to have the opportunity of raising three young gorillas together. The arrival of Albert, Bouba and Bata meant that San Diego was also the first zoo to possess a potential breeding trio of the primate that is possibly humankind's closest living relative. At that time no gorillas had ever been born in captivity. Of the three infants whose combined weight was only 20 pounds, Albert at three months of age was the youngest and smallest. Unable to sit up by himself, he had to be content with watching the world from the confines of his crib for the first few months.

Albert's popularity in print through the years has made him a Zoo ambassador of world fame. From cute baby pictures in *Parade Magazine* to recent photos as a magnificent silverback in scientific texts, he has represented the genus *Gorilla* and the San Diego Zoo.

Even in death, Albert will continue to educate and bring enjoyment to the public. Shortly after his death, Albert began the journey to the Denver Museum of Natural History. In the Museum's new tropical African diorama, he will resume the role of star attraction which he played so well during his lifetime at the San Diego Zoo.

## By Michaele M. Robinson

*Harold Mitchell was honored by Society trustees for his performance as Master Keeper, especially on behalf of Albert during his long illness. Michaele Robinson, Zoo librarian, offers Mitch's memories of his favorite charge.*

**February 1979**

In February 1971 Master Keeper Harold "Mitch" Mitchell became the keeper primarily responsible for the care of the Zoo's great apes. This includes the pigmy chimpanzees, orangutans, and gorillas. Mitch has a special relationship with each of his charges, as do many keepers.

"I noticed Albert had been slowing down considerably the last two years, which I attributed to old age. He started eating less, becoming lethargic and listless. His arthritis seemed to be giving him more trouble. He was given aspirin, which helped for a while."

In early June, Albert was taken to the Zoo hospital for a complete physical examination. At that time heart failure was diagnosed, and he was given medication to help relieve his symptoms.

"He rallied for a while, and was placed back on exhibit. He was eating well during this time, but never regained the weight he had lost earlier. The week before he died, Albert would not eat his evening meal, so he was fed outdoors to try to get him to eat more. During this week he started to look heavier, probably from the edema. He wouldn't eat much at all, but he did take his medications, which were

*Albert bares his teeth.*

mixed in with baby food. He liked aspirin tablets and ate them readily.

"Animals can often communicate to us if we are observant enough to interpret their actions," says Mitch. His favorite experience with Albert occurred when instead of the usual small aspirin tablets given Albert in the morning and evening, an especially large tablet was tried. "With the regular aspirins, Albert would reach through the bars and take them out of my hand. But with the large tablets he would take one out of my hand and then drop it on the floor. I would pick it up and place it back in my hand, and he would take it and drop it again. Occasionally he would put one in his mouth and spit it out. Finally he must have become exasperated trying to get the point across that he didn't like those big aspirins. The next time I placed a tablet in my hand and waited for him to pick it up, he grabbed my hand and held on for a while. Because his hand was so big, I was able to slide mine out rather easily, I understood. I gave him his regular aspirins, which he gently picked out of my hand and proceeded to eat."

## By Edalee Harwell

*Edalee Harwell became surrogate mother to baby Albert and his two sisters, and was primarily responsible for their care and training through infancy and early childhood. (See "Gorilla Notes," pages 82/83).*

### February 1979

When hints of the existence of a giant man-like ape in darkest Africa burst upon the scientific scene in the 1850s, it became inevitable that attempts would be made to bring them back to astound civilization. It was tried time and again, but only infant gorillas could be taken alive and all soon died. By 1915 the director of the Bronx Zoo prophesied that an adult gorilla would never be seen alive in any zoo. In 1932 the London Zoo declared that they had decided to abandon all attempts at keeping gorillas.

The picture was changing by the time Albert and the females Bouba and Bata arrived in San Diego in August 1949. Although this marked the first time that any zoo had been able to try raising three gorillas together, there was no longer a mystery as to how to care for them. They were treated like human infants.

When a New York animal dealer cabled that he had three baby lowland gorillas, he admitted they were so tiny and sick that it required round-the-clock care to keep them alive. The females were probably only a few months

older than Albert so all still had bottles of formula and were bathed with baby oil.

With sweet orange-flavored vitamin syrup as an incentive, Albert soon learned to handle a spoon by himself, and all three later ate their mush and baby food using a spoon and bowl. They drank their milk and juice from cups. They were protected as much as possible from the infant diseases of civilization and all had their sugar cubes with polio vaccine.

Since this was before the Children's Zoo was built the gorillas lived in an upstairs room at the Zoo hospital. When they outgrew the cribs, they moved to a sunny corner room provided with individual sleeping cages and a large fenced play area, with bars for climbing.

*Albert in a pensive mood.*

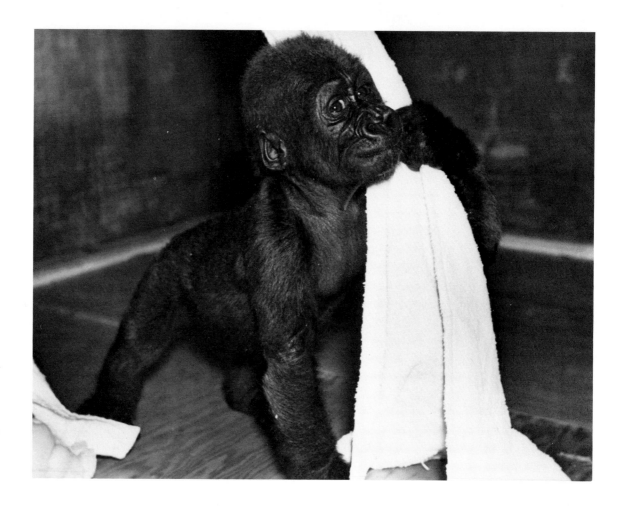

*Young Albert and his security blanket.*

An enclosure was constructed in the hospital backyard which held tire swings, ropes, a teeter-totter, and a metal slide. The young gorillas delighted in charging up the slide, stamping their feet to make all the noise possible. Occasional disagreements brought warning "coughs" or ear-splitting screams that seemed impossible coming from such small individuals. Best of all was when they could get their human friends to swing them by the hand, to chase them or tickle them. Accepting the responsibilities of a potential gorilla troop leader, Albert always approached anything new with caution. One day he discovered an inchworm on a leaf and carefully avoided that corner of the cage for the rest of the day. He disdained a new rubber doll, although Bata delighted in tossing it about, and Bouba gave it a drubbing by tucking it under her chin, then beating her chest.

By the time they were approaching maturity it had been discovered that raising the three together was not the way to develop a reproducing gorilla unit. Although they were actually unrelated, they had grown up as brother and sisters instead of potential mates. Following the completion of a new gorilla grotto at the Zoo in June 1963, some changes were made. Bata, least compatible of the three, was sent to the zoo in Fort Worth, Texas, which needed a companion for its male. Joining Albert and Bouba in the new San Diego enclosure were Vila and Trib, both graduates of the Children's Zoo.

The move was crowned with success in the birth of Alvila, daughter of Albert and Vila. Born June 3, 1965, she was the first for the Zoo, and only the seventh captive-bred gorilla to survive anywhere in the world.

Albert's popularity and the success of the gorilla colony at the San Diego Zoo have pointed the way toward keeping gorillas in large groups, as is being done at the Wild Animal Park

# The Vulture Who Came in from the Cold

## By Sheldon Campbell

*Sheldon Campbell, in common with the vulture he describes, is an authority on defying man-made barriers. He admits that his lifelong involvement with the San Diego Zoo, most recently as its president, began when as a teenager he climbed its fences to avoid paying the admission charge.*

**October 1982**

Some animals actually try to get in to, not out of, the San Diego Wild Animal Park. Instead of seeking the freedom to soar or roam unrestrained, these refugees from the wild seem to be looking for a room with a view, three square meals a day, a good hospital and medical plan, and protection from men with poisons and guns.

The most recent volunteer for captivity was a common turkey vulture, one of several attracted by the Park's newest structure, the "condormimium," built for the purpose of breeding highly endangered California condors.

Rather than see the condorminium's six large, wire-covered apartments stand vacant while awaiting the capture of California condors, Art Risser, general curator of birds, and his staff decided they would study aspects of condor husbandry with some stand-ins. Consequently, four of the apartments were filled with relatives—two adult Andean condors and two juveniles, two king vultures, two turkey vultures, and four black vultures.

Each apartment in the condorminium is sizeable, embracing 3,200 square feet of ground space, and is high enough at 22 feet to allow even the gigantic condors to fly. Near a center service corridor each apartment has a bedroom with a balcony; both are sheltered from wind and rain. Altogether, with prime roosting trees, green grass and vines, wading pools, and a magnificent view of the San Pasqual Valley—these units have all the

*The condorminium at the Wild Animal Park.*

*A black vulture roosts on a convenient cactus limb.*

amenities, or apparently so thought the volunteer turkey vulture.

He was one of twelve wild vultures who gathered to roost on the condorminium after it was first occupied in December 1981. When they were not soaring above, these vultures sat in the sun atop the poles which support the wire mesh exterior of the structure. Occasionally, keepers swear, the two turkey vultures on the inside passed tidbits of food to their wild brethren.

On a gray morning when the ground mist still clung in the vicinity of the condorminium, Keeper William Toone came early, as usual, to care for his charges.

First he had to unlock the gates of the high peripheral fence, topped with barbed wire, which is designed to keep out predators or curious people. Next Toone had to unlock the main entrance of the condorminium. This wirecovered door leads into an antechambeer which has a second door on the inner side—an arrangement to prevent escapes by assuring that one of the two doors will always be closed.

As Toone entered the antechamber, he glanced into the apartment housing the two juvenile Andean condors. With sudden shock he saw that there were three birds in the apartment, the two which were supposed to be there and a stranger. The third bird was a turkey vulture. Nor did the stranger wear a band as do the other turkey vultures.

The only explanation was fantastic! The bird had broken in. But how?

Close examination revealed the route—under the front door into the antechamber, under a wire partition into a feeding chamber, and from there into the apartment. The Andean condors paid no attention to their new roommate. All three birds roosted quite contentedly within a few feet of one another.

One cannot, of course, probe the innermost thoughts of a turkey vulture, if, indeed, the bird has innermost thoughts. Yet one must speculate that the newly captive vulture has no desire to rejoin his free brothers and sisters circling or roosting outside. Every day of the year they must spend hours soaring above the earth, with sharp eyes scanning hill and dale below in constant search for scraps of carrion. Meanwhile, he inside has especially prepared diets brought to him, the company of kin, and the opportunity, whenever he wants, to exercise his wings.

Like some human beings who value security above all else, he has escaped from freedom.

(preceding page) Epiphyllum

(this page) Day lily (Hemerocallis)

(opposite page) Coelogyne orchid
(Coelogyne cristata alba)

(following page) Mexican bush sage
(Salvia leucantha)

# The Northern Sea Elephant

## By Charles R. Schroeder, D.V.M.

*Dr. Charles Schroeder, executive director emeritus, made one of his rare appearances in ZOONOOZ with this report of a 1933 expedition to study the Northern sea elephant. Ironically, the method described, destroying the animal in order to study it, would not be sanctioned by today's wildlife conservationists—of whom Dr. Schroeder has long been a leader.*

**March 1934**

For a number of years the San Diego Zoological Society has conducted expeditions to Guadalupe Island for the purpose of obtaining live specimens of the Northern sea elephant to be used as exhibits in the Zoo. The greater number were unsuccessfully kept in captivity, their average life in the Zoo seldom exceeded a year. The lack of success was given to various causes such as improper diet, failure to supply water of the same composition as sea water, heavy nematode infestations, gastric ulcers and disease of bacterial origin. Statistics are of little value where a definite knowledge of the normal picture is not available. It was our intention to compare our morbid pathological statistics with the destroyed normal sea elephant in his natural habitat.

On May 29th we anchored off Elephant Seal beach, Guadalupe Island. There was a noticable increase in number of specimens on the beach over earlier expeditions. We estimated four hundred males on the beach at our first visit, varied ages, yearlings to aged bulls. This beach was free of females at this season. A three-quarters grown bull was selected as a specimen to be destroyed. He was quite easily approached and driven above the high water mark to a convenient area where a tent fly could be erected to shield him from the sun during the process of skinning, skeletonizing and posting. The animal was opened and

posted. Tissue was cut for histologic section and the stomach contents were noted. Six pounds of stones from 1/8 inch to 1 1/2 inch diameter and kelp were found together with some squid hooks. The stomach demonstrated numerous scars on the gastic mucosa representing the remains of healed ulcers. Neither acute lesions or parasites were found.

We were particularly interested in collecting data which had not been recorded and satisfactorily explained. Unilateral blindness is common, in all probability the result of trauma induced by the coarse sharp larval sand on the beach. Bilateral blindness was seen but apparently these specimens were unable to seek out sufficient food to survive.

The caterpillar-like form of locomotion and peculiar guttural-like trumpeting of the males makes a weird spectacle to behold. Many males have immense scars, in all probability the result of attacks by natural enemies and not the result of combat within their own group. The fighting males often lunged at each other, inflicting puncture wounds, but at no time did they lacerate the skin nor does the structure of their canines indicate that they are capable of delivering a wound the dimension of those we observed.

Males approach each other cautiously. When close enough, they raise themselves on their fore flippers and lunge at each other with canines exposed, proboscis thrown back, often producing minor skin punctures on the thick armored coat of the shoulder and neck. Three minutes, and never more than five, completely exhaust the animals. The combatants lie side by side temporarily forgetting their animosities and spend a recuperating period very much in excess of the period of combat.

When approaching the water every advantage is taken of the surf. The body is extended head straight forward and held close to the sand as the wave breaks over them. As the water recedes they raise their hind flippers and are pushed seaward, head erect, by the returning swell.

When reaching water sufficiently deep, then they submerge and continue out to sea, coming to the surface beyond the surf, there to loaf in the swell for indefinite periods.

# Gorilla Notes

## By Edalee Harwell

*Edalee Harwell was hospital secretary when three baby lowland gorillas arrived in 1949. At the time little was known about the rearing of young gorillas. Given the responsibility, Harwell described the learning experience—for all concerned—in a series of reports of which these are excerpts.*

**March-May 1951**

Gorillas love rain. At least the Zoo's big gorillas, Mbongo and Ngagi, used to seem to. Sometimes they would even refuse to go into their sleeping quarters to be shut up for the night, preferring to stay out all night to play in the rain.

Bata, Bouba and Albert, the Zoo's present gorilla trio, had no opinions on the subject. They had never been out in the rain! Of course, it had rained in Africa, but they were such tiny babies when they were captured and brought to America that it is doubtful that they could remember it.

It was a perfect day for the introduction. The drizzle was steady, but light and warm. We led them downstairs and out the door into the backyard.

They all realized immediately that something was going on. Albert kept looking up, blinking and screwing up his face as the drops spattered down. He seemed to be trying to locate the source. Bouba tugged at my hand, trying to lead me over to a little clump of bushes where she could get under cover. Bata went to first one and then the other of us, raising her arms to be picked up. When we all refused, Bata went back up the steps to the hospital and began working at the door knob. The others hurried over eagerly. All had obviously had enough and were ready to go in.

On stormy days, they stay inside in the new cage especially built for them in the Gorilla Room. The cage takes up three-fourths of the room. The gorillas like it because there is a supporting center pole and two horizontal braces, all ideal for swinging and climbing.

Last week it was reported to me that Bouba had a new and amazing stunt which she had perfected: hanging from one of the horizontal bars by her feet! Naturally, I wanted to see her do it. I spent as much time as possible in the Gorilla Room, observing and waiting. But never once did she even approach the bar.

Then yesterday she gave in. Suddenly Bouba climbed to the horizontal bar, walked sloth-fashion along it and let herself down to hang by her feet. She dangled a moment, beating her chest, then pulled herself back up to the bar and slid down the pole to the floor.

A few minutes later Albert climbed up to the horizontal bar and started across it, balancing on all fours. This is one of his favorite tricks. This time, however, he lost his balance in the middle, swayed violently from side to side, and finally swung down under the bar. He paused a moment, then let go with both hands—and he, too, was hanging by his feet.

Albert didn't pull himself up again as Bouba had. He dropped head first. Instead of crashing to the floor, as I expected, he landed on his hands, then collapsed limply and rolled as he fell, like an experienced tumbler. Obviously, he had been practicing.

When I clapped, Albert stood up and clapped too, then ran to the bar to do it all over again. He spent the entire afternoon hanging and falling for anyone and everyone who wanted to watch, applauding for himself after each time.

Bata has always been the largest of the three. Not until lately, however, has she consciously taken advantage of her physical superiority. Now she has reached the teasing

*Bata, Bouba and Albert.*

stage. She has found what fun it is to give Albert or Bouba a hard push, then run. Sometimes she gets Albert so upset and angry that he shrieks whenever she comes near him.

Bata teases to get attention as much as anything, and a reprimand appears to be as satisfying as praise. Ignored, she redoubles her efforts; spanked, she waits until our backs are turned.

The problem will solve itself eventually. As soon as Albert is able to do some pushing around on his own and can prove that he is as rough or rougher than she is, she will stop her nonsense. Even now Albert doesn't take her teasing passively. Sometimes he gets so furious that he lunges at her again and again, really trying to hurt her. She just knocks him down, runs over him and drags him around by an arm or leg. But one of these days Albert will get her down and bite her convincingly, and from then on she'll be a good gorilla.

Luckily, Bouba, Bata and Albert are not problem children all of the time. Most of the time they are winning, amusing little personalities. Bouba especially gets extremely sentimental. While she is being groomed, she will put her arms up to be hugged time and again. She also likes to be rocked and will put her arms around your neck and rock from side to side until you get the idea and will rock her in return. Once I saw her throw her arms around Albert's neck and proceed to rock him gently. He soon decided that was sissy stuff and left her abruptly to go wrestle with Bata.

Then there was the time that Bata did the unforgivable. She jumped out of her chair at lunchtime and went running off. I gave her a sound paddling and plunked her back in the chair to finish her meal.

Apparently Bouba had watched the proceedings with interest. A moment later I heard a peculiar thumping noise and turned to see Bouba giving Albert a good old-fashioned spanking. Albert turned his back and took it— just another game as far as he was concerned.

Patting and beating seem to be the natural thing to do for gorillas. Chest, tummy, foot and floor pounding is an inherent part of all their play activities. Sometimes they even stand and beat their inner thighs, and whack one inner elbow with the other hand.

I have never seen any of them beat their chests with their fists; cupped hands make a much more satisfactory noise. However, they do use their knuckles to drum on the floor, and I have seen Albert gently knocking on his head with both fists—trying to knock some sense into it, possibly.

Albert frequently will stand up and pound out a rapid tattoo on his chest, syncopating it with alternate stampings of his feet. A favorite game starts with Albert sitting on the floor

*Harwell administers medicine to Albert.*

and one of us opposite him, both patting the floor in between. Gradually, the tempo becomes more frantic and is supplemented by his stamping feet. Finally, he is banging the floor violently with fists and feet and wagging his head in time, with his mouth stretched wide and eyes tightly shut.

Going to the other extreme, he sometimes taps the floor with both forefingers, making scarcely any noise at all. Several times I have seen him tapping his forefingers gently together, and once he poked his fingers through the screen and tapped them together outside the cage.

When Bouba and Bata put their arms around us for a little cuddling, they frequently accompany the squeezes with gentle pats. Unlike the usual patting, they keep the heel of the hand quiet and just pat with their fingers like a human mother comforting her child. I would be tremendously interested to know if gorilla mothers comfort their babies in this fashion, too.

There are a million and one other interesting questions to be answered about gorillas, and Bouba, Bata and Albert have already shown promise of eventually helping to clear up many of the mysteries surrounding their fabulous tribe.

# Understanding Koalas

## By J.L. Throp

*Koalas and the Zoo have a long-running relationship; for many years we were the only zoo outside Australia to exhibit the furry marsupials. Likewise, Jack Throp and the Zoo go back a long way. He began his career in San Diego. He is now director of Sydney's Taronga Zoo from where, surrounded by koalas, he ventured this anthropomorphic view.*

**September 1981**

Nobody really believes that koalas hate Qantas. My experience with koalas is that they probably haven't given Qantas a thought. I'd say they haven't thought of Continental, Pan American, British Airways, or any other airlines, either. In fact one would be hard put to prove that koalas think much about anything.

What is it then about koalas, that has so attracted people? Most people have never seen a koala, but almost everybody knows of them and readily identifies with a photograph.

San Diego Zoo is the only zoo outside Australia where they can be seen. The government of Australia long had a ban on export of the animals so that no other zoo could receive them. Then why has San Diego Zoo been so lucky?

A few other zoos have had koalas in the past but only San Diego and San Francisco Zoos have had sufficient varieties of eucalyptus to enable the animals to survive. These two zoos received koalas in 1959 as a gift from Sir Edward Hallstrom, then director of Taronga Zoo, Sydney. The San Francisco animals were eventually sent to San Diego. (San Diego also received koalas in 1925, 1928, 1952, again in 1976, and most recently in 1981).

There is hope now that koalas might be seen in a few other zoos around the world as the Australian Government has recently abolished the export ban. Koalas, lyrebirds, and platypuses are no longer classified as endangered. Nevertheless, very exacting conditions must be met by the importing foreign zoos.

The difficulty of keeping koalas will limit the distribution outside Australia, yet the animal will remain one of zoodom's most prized exhibits because they are so pleasing to look at, even if they are only sitting in the fork of a tree. People get ecstatic if they are fortunate enough to see one move. Koalas look like cuddly stuffed toys. They *are* stuffed too, with eucalyptus leaves, thousands of them.

Koalas are generally called koala bears by misinformed people, due to the koala's teddy-bear appearance. Koalas are marsupials and are in no way related to bears. Still, they look like bears, teddy bears at least, and people's minds are not easily reckoned with.

Recently an American tourist approached the Taronga Zoo Information Centre and asked directions to see "those cute little qantases." The guide was temporarily set back but recovered quickly. "Down that pathway, turn to the right, look for a building named Koala, that's where the qantases are."

Australians are by no means blasé about koalas. It is a fact that in the Sydney suburbs the value of real estate is immeasurably enhanced if a koala is living on the property.

Something should be said about koala sex life. It can't be much because they only mate once a year. In New South Wales this social interaction is consummated some time in the months from September through January.

After a very short period of gestation, 35 days, a single naked fetus is born, about three-quarters of an inch in length. The fetus attaches to one of the two nipples in the pouch and settles down to do some growing.

Six months pass before it first appears over the rim for a look around. By this time the infant is approximately 7 inches in length. The youngster fiddles around in the pouch for

*Gumdrop drinking from a cup.*

*Gumdrop arrived at the Zoo still in his mother's pouch.*

two more months, sticking its head out more and more frequently for a breath of fresh air, before finally emerging.

From then on it is seen riding on its mother's back in double-decker koala style. The baby is weaned at one year and is living entirely on eucalyptus leaves by that time. Life after that is a placid 16 to 20 years with once-a-year moments of ecstasy.

Nature's biggest threat to koala security is the bush fire, which can sweep through vast areas of koala habitat and kill everything in its path. The bush needs this for regeneration, and in a roundabout way it probably even helps koalas by stimulating new food-tree growth.

Man was a dire threat for a time; there was a passion for koala skin coats. Fortunately, the government stepped in and made koalas a protected species before there was total destruction of the scattered populations.

I suppose the remaining threat from man is still to be reasoned with—that's the threat of being hugged to death. Talk to any overseas visitor and you will quickly learn that he or she has a mad desire to squeeze a koala. Think what damage a million visitors a year to Australia could do if they went around squeezing koalas. Fortunately, there is no subject that gets a placid koala so stirred up as that of being squeezed. They come out of their trees with tooth and nail flaying. Shredded tourist.

For a koala to be safely handled it must be trained from its youth not to use its teeth and claws. The koala must learn that people are very tender-barked trees that get all mushy inside when a koala gets among their branches.

There is a little training required of the visitor as well. Firstly, the would-be recipient of the koala must put his or her arms down and pretend to be a tree trunk. After the koala climbs the tree, the tourist is encouraged to raise one arm and support the bottom end of the animal. The visitor may then gently stroke the animal with the free hand and encourage somebody, quickly, to get a picture.

From the koala's point of view this becomes an inconvenience. Koalas are accustomed to selecting a nice fork in a tree as a resting place and settling in for hours at a time. The usual tourist is only good for a few minutes, then has to run and catch a bus.

Koalas trained to tolerate handling find that their nap is divided into dozens of short segments while cameras are clicking and whirring. Koalas might wonder where do all those tourists come from? There seems an endless supply of hopeful koala huggers.

# Our Frozen Zoo

## By Suzanne Hansen

*Is there life after death? Yes—in a manner of speaking—if the Zoo research department's efforts to preserve living cells for future use is considered. Suzanne Hansen, cytogenetics and molecular genetics technician, describes the how and why of this exciting technique.*

**February 1981**

Dr. Kurt Benirschke, research director, displays vials of cells from The Frozen Zoo.

Considerable publicity has been focused on the research department's Frozen Zoo. But just what is that mysterious facility? In a sense it is exactly what the term says, a collection of frozen animals, but it is not a huge icy room of frozen tigers and tapirs.

Rather, it is two washing-machine-sized stainless steel chests containing box upon box of small plastic vials. In those vials are minuscule amounts of the most basic and precious substance—living cells. The skin cells of nearly 350 different animals from 120 species are maintained in these liquid nitrogen freezers at a temperature of $-196°C$ ($-384.8°F$), as well as semen and embryos from a number of species.

How are these cells collected and subsequently frozen to be kept alive indefinitely in an overgrown ice chest? Skin cells are obtained initially as skin biopsies or ear notches, taken only while the animal is anesthetized for veterinary treatment, or for shipment, or if the animal has died.

The 3 to 4mm square of skin is dissected into tiny pieces and placed in a sterile flask where it is allowed to attach to the surface of the flask. A rich liquid medium much like mother's chicken soup and containing all the necessary elements for cellular growth covers the pieces of skin, which in one to two weeks begin to sprout fibroblasts of skin cells.

After these cells proliferate to a quantity of about eight million, the cells are removed from the flasks and diluted with a medium containing a freezing protectant. The chemical protectant prevents the cells from bursting as a result of the internal formation of ice crystals during the freezing process. This mixture of cells, medium, and protectant is pipetted into vials and then placed in a freezing apparatus which gradually ($1°C$ per minute) lowers the temperature of the cells from $4°C$ ($40°F$) to $-50°C$ ($-122°F$). At this point the vials are ready to be stored in the liquid nitrogen freezers.

Ova flushed from the uteri of females under study for breeding enhancement, and semen collected by electroejaculation are frozen immediately after they are collected. The fertilized ova, which can be as small as two cells or as large as several hundred cells (blastocyst), are frozen in a similar manner to skin cells, except the rate of freezing depends on the species.

Semen, on the other hand, requires an extender or a very specific freezing fluid designed to dilute and protect the fragile sperm within the semen. The composition of the extender varies greatly depending on the species being frozen, as semen from one species may be a viscous gel whereas in another it may be fluid. Glycerol and fresh egg yolk are two examples of extenders. The subsequent freezing procedure for semen is essentially the same as that for skin cells.

For what purposes are cells withdrawn and thawed from our cell bank? Skin cells are analyzed for their genetic content and are used in many genetic and hereditary studies by members of our research department and other investigators. Additionally, the bank contains all of the hereditary material potentially useful to future scientists in studying species whose survival is currently in jeopardy.

Ova are being implanted into females of the same species which may be more able to sustain pregnancies, or they are transferred into other closely related and less endangered species for incubation and birth.

Semen is used for artificial insemination into females which at the time the ejaculate was collected were not receptive to the male. Also, frozen semen can be sent to other zoos for artificial insemination in animals difficult to transport, which will further increase and enhance the breeding population.

The Frozen Zoo. Perhaps the best definition of it is a treasure chest of one of our greatest treasures—animal life.

# Problems in Testing an Adult Male Gorilla

## By Duane M. Rumbaugh, Ph.D.

*Dr. Duane Rumbaugh, at the time professor of psychology at San Diego State University, conducted a five-year study on the learning abilities of the Zoo's primates. One of his most challenging encounters was with Albert, the Zoo's famed lowland gorilla.*

**February 1965**

Preparing to test the learning ability of Albert, a sterling 250-pound specimen of the lowland gorilla, has resulted in a contest between the temperament of beast and the insistence of man.

Interest in testing the learning ability of Albert stems from the study program that was initiated in 1960 to define the relative learning abilities of apes and monkeys as represented in the primate collection of the San Diego Zoo.

Until last year, the study had been restricted to very young animals, but with the construction of the new grottos it became possible to study adult specimens as well. Each grotto includes two test stations adjoining the rooms to which the animals retire at night for food, rest, and shelter. It is in one of these stations in the gorilla grotto that Albert, now fifteen years old, has had his recent confrontation with the academics.

As with people, it is to be expected that mature animals will do better than very young ones. Accordingly, the study of adult animals is important. But before the ability to learn can be inferred by performance on a variety of tasks, it is necessary to adapt each animal to the demands of the test situation and its routine. Some animals adapt very rapidly to the experimental situation with its unusual noises and isolation and learn within a few minutes how to displace the bins in order to gain access to the food. On the other hand, some animals are very problematical, requiring several months to adapt to these conditions. Albert has proven himself to be the most trying case to date.

My first attempt to adapt Albert to the experimental situation was an invigorating one, as it became immediately apparent that Albert was going to be very open and frank about his reactions. The test apparatus includes a steel door that is lowered for the presentation of a trial, then raised for preparation of the next trial so as to keep placement of objects and rewards from the animal's view. When this door was lowered the first time, Albert commenced beating his chest, ran toward the apparatus, and hit the bin on his extreme left with a force sufficient to break a brass locking pin.

On September 25, conditions seemed appropriate for starting Albert on the first discrimination problem. This problem simply is that of a red square and a red circle. Choice of the square results in food reward; choice of the circle results in an empty food well.

On the first presentation of this problem, Albert handled himself well. His response was to the square and it resulted in reward. On the second trial, however, he made an error by choosing the circle. Likewise, on the third trial he made an error, and then his composure shattered. He looked twice at the middle bin (which was empty), backed up, and while holding down the steel door with his left hand, socked the bin to the right—the impact almost threw the circle up and out.

On the following days I tried to adapt Albert to the experience of getting rewarded only now and then for pushing the empty bins, the thought being that it was the frustration of nonrewarded responses that irritated him. Progress was made in this to the point that the square and circle discrimination problem was reintroduced. Upon doing so his behavior again became completely emotional, including vocalizations that resembled a staccato "hoot." It was clear that Albert was not given to making decisions—in fact, it appeared that he would rather fight than decide between the square and the circle.

Though I tried never to press Albert beyond the point that made him tense, at times I obviously miscalculated. Gradually, I became acutely aware of the stances and facial expressions that signaled growing tension and imminent displays. Occasionally large beads of perspiration would break out on his face, and it invariably meant that his test-oriented behaviors were about to deteriorate. At these times Albert would exude a pungent odor that defies the written word.

By October 20, events led me to reluctantly conclude that the test situation would have to be radically altered if there were to be hope of eventually testing Albert. His habits of both holding and slamming down the door on the apparatus had become perfected to the point that we had exchanged roles—he was now the one defining how the testing was to be conducted, while I had been relegated to the role of responder.

The apparatus had to be modified to

*Albert regards the camera as he does researchers, with skepticism.*

immobilize the bins and all other parts that Albert could move or knock about. Now the plan was to have Albert indicate his choice of objects by just putting his hand on the front of the bin containing his choice.

To implement this plan it was first necessary to teach Albert that the sound of a soft buzzer signaled delivery of food, the reward for correct choices. But Albert did not respond favorably and soon he even refused to accept food delivered this way. In seconds his reluctance turned to protest; he began to "hoot," then hit the bin on his left with alarming force. Inspection revealed that the glass front of the bin had been shattered. The imprint of his left fist remained, with relatively clear definition of the outline of his thumbnail and the hair on the back of his hand. Albert's hand showed no injury, and he gave no sign of discomfort.

I secured the apparatus and went around to the bars of Albert's room and said in a low voice, "What's the trouble, Albert?"

His response seemed deliberate as he stood on all fours with his head low. With his hand he then offered me a well-chewed piece of orange peel. When he dropped it through the bars for me, I picked it up and offered him a sprig of bamboo. After all, there was nothing personal about the incident.

The exchange of objects was complete, and it was only one of the many more to come. On some days it seemed that there was nothing that Albert had that was too good for me, and I received peels, fruit stems, portions of bamboo, and other foods, each deftly slipped to me through a slot in the apparatus.

And so the contest continues—the nature of the brute pitted against the wit of man, with both represented in equal portions, it would seem. I have become an important figure in Albert's life, and he now recognizes me from afar, regardless of what my clothing might be. Unfortunately, I know nothing more about Albert's learning ability now than I did the first of September.

# The Bizarre Bezoar

## By William B. Karesh, D.V.M.

*Ever heard of a bezoar? Few ZOONOOZ readers had until Dr. William B. Karesh, a 1983 veterinary intern, shed some light on the strange stones found in the stomachs of hoofed animals, and the equally strange uses they can be put to.*

**July 1983**

Many know of the crystalline formations causing gall stones or kidney and bladder stones, but few have heard of the bezoars found in hoofed animals. A bezoar is a stone formed from layers of minerals being deposited around a central core. Such stones are sometimes found in the stomachs or intestines of animals, including man.

Bezoars have been known to man since ancient times. Once thought to have medicinal powers and to be infallible antidotes, these stones may have received their name from the Arabic word badizohr, which means antidote.

Throughout the Middle Ages bezoars were highly valued as talismans and remedies against infectious diseases—plague, for example—and for the treatment of intestinal worms, cramps, fever, and fainting. Stones from animals of the Middle East and Orient were available in 17th and 18th century pharmacies as oriental bezoars, as opposed to the occidental ones obtained from llamas, vicunas, and alpacas of the west. Princes had them set in gold and silver and had drinking vessels

*Kunsthistorisches Museum, Vienna*

*Bezoar on a stand supported by lions.*

*Bezoar rests on a stand of gold and tiger cowry shell.*

*Kunsthistorisches Museum, Vienna*

*Bezoar fashioned into a covered cup, from the court of Kaiser Rudolf II.*

made from them. Bezoars set in gold and trimmed with emeralds and rubies during the 16th century are on display in the Kunsthistorisches Museum in Vienna, Austria.

Most true bezoars are found in the stomachs of ruminant animals, those animals having a 3- or 4-compartment stomach which acts like a fermentation vat, as in cattle, sheep, and goats. Most wild hoofed animals, or ungulates, would fall into this category.

Horses are not ruminants but sometimes form stones nearly the size of bowling balls in their large intestines. These stones are different in chemical composition from most bezoars and are called enteroliths (enteron is the Greek word for intestine and litho is Greek for stone). Bezoars have been found in antelopes, gazelles, cameloids, cattle, sheep, and goats.

At the San Diego Zoo and the Wild Animal Park, bezoars have been found during the routine post-mortem examinations of Kenya impala, a llama, and a Nilgiri tahr, all of which died of other causes.

Usually a bezoar will stay in the large rumen of an animal and never cause a problem, but, rarely, the mass will move to another area and block the passage of food and water. This happened to Rowdy, a male llama reared at the Zoo. His keeper noticed that he wasn't behaving normally; within a day or two his appetite had decreased, and he was apparently constipated. Laxatives had no effect so Rowdy was brought to the hospital for a physical. He was sedated and X-rays were taken with new radiographic equipment donated by the Naval Hospital.

A large mass was visible in Rowdy's stomach. Surgery was performed, and a two-to three-inch bezoar was removed from the outflow tract of the stomach. The stone was composed of concentric layers of calcium compounds surrounding a 3/4-inch core of hair and plant fibers.

Rowdy eventually succumbed to postoperative complications but left us with the skills and knowledge to diagnose and treat this problem before debilitation or death.

*Bob as a youngster.*

# Bob Orangutan . . .
# From a Sarawak
# Jungle to a
# College Education

## By Christopher E. Parker, Ph.D.

*Some experts believe that the orangutan may be the smartest of the great apes and Zoo personnel who have attempted to keep the ingenious animals confined would support that opinion. Dr. Christopher Parker, who participated in a study of the comparative intelligence of the primates, drew his own conclusions.*

**March 1969**

On Christmas day of 1956, the curator of the Sarawak Museum on the island of Borneo dropped a cuddly little ball of red fur on his wife's bed—a present to help shake off the doldrums which accompany the common cold. Little did Tom and Barbara Harrisson know how greatly their lives would be altered by this event or how much the fate of the wild orangutan would be elevated. That cuddly ball of fur was Bob. The "beautiful baby with dark brown eyes," as Barbara Harrisson put it, had been confiscated by a forest guard when found living in a Dayak long-house after his mother had been shot. Bob was between one and two years old and not more than fifteen pounds.

Bob was at first caged in a small roofed-in platform outside the bathroom of the Harrisson's home. When first let out of his cage, Bob "raced madly away, head over heels on the lawn," to dance, stand upright, and wave his arms. He was constantly picking at fruit, leaves, bits of loose wire, wood, and loose shingles, and endlessly fiddling with all sorts of things. Door locking mechanisms were his specialty.

One of his cherished pastimes was walking quietly about the garden with Barbara. He also enjoyed eating, in fact, "eating was Bob's principal occupation." But Bob's greatest delight was playing with the tree branches supplied to him daily. He was constantly bending and twisting the branches, peeling off the bark, stripping leaves, then carrying them about, usually poking for insects. He used branches to make elaborate structures, "tied" branches and swing rope together into enormous tangled messes. It is any wonder that today, eleven years later, Bob is still somewhat of a mechanical genius?

Bob stayed with the Harrissons for eighteen months before traveling to San Diego, given to the Zoo by the Harrissons as a mate for Noell. Robella, born two and one-half years ago, was the eventual result of that pairing.

When Bob left Sarawak, he was a three-year-old, 35-pound, strong, playful "baby" with definite mechanical inclinations and an over-powering sense of curiosity. On the very first evening, an urgent call from the nursery attendant, revealed that Bob was taking his cage apart by untwisting the heavy wire links. An emergency repair job lasted barely to morning which found him diligently working his way out by another route.

A bigger and stronger cage proved little more of a challenge to his skill. Once out, he promptly made a hole in a nearby penguin cage. By now Bob probably thought it was all a wonderful new game; so when put into a heavy barred cage used to hold bears and lions he continued the sport, and spent the night in the feed room. Amiable Bob didn't seem to mind being led gently and quietly back to a cage after each escape.

A year later Bob entered a school on the Zoo grounds along with Noell Orangutan, Howie and Lucy Chimpanzee, and Vila Gorilla. This was no ordinary school nor was it a trade school designed to teach seal-like tricks. It was an extension of San Diego State College directed by Professor Duane Rumbaugh.

In the early studies, Bob was certainly not at the head of the class. He did not adapt well to the experimental situation, becoming more indifferent as the novelty wore off. He finally became a drop-out and was allowed to mature for three years before being tested again.

As it turned out, he was not much more successful as an adult than as a juvenile. After testing five orangutans, Professor Rumbaugh

*Young orangutans.*

Janet Hawes

*It runs in the family. Ken Allen, Bob's son, has inherited his father's ingenuity and tool-using skills. To the delight of press and public – and the consternation of his keepers – Ken Allen has managed to escape on several occasions from his supposedly secure enclosure. In this 1982 photo, in which he appears bent on chipping his way out of a previous exhibit, he provides a revealing glimpse of his spirit and determination.*

found Bob still at the bottom of the class. It was obvious that poor performance in discrimination learning problems was not characteristic of all the orangutans as three others were performing well.

Professor Rumbaugh concluded that, perhaps, "as orangs age in captive situations, they lose whatever motivations are necessary for sustaining attention and cooperation in formal learning set testing situations." He continued, "There is no reason to believe that Bob was, in fact, a particularly inept learner, for he had a remarkable record of dismantling cages."

It is characteristic of Bob to show more interest in the research support facilities—the apparatus, equipment, tools, and the experimenter—than in the task itself.

Bob was idle again for nearly three years before I began a study of manipulation and tool-using in apes. The first measurement situation consisted of an aluminum object tethered by a chain inside a box; it was intended to gain some idea of the variety of ways the object would be manipulated. Bob's interest was immediately captured by the complex, movable object. His interest was so intense that the object was torn out by the roots and the box reduced to plywood hash.

Undaunted, we built another, stronger box (in three days), used heavier chain to secure the object, and tried again. Just as undaunted, Bob took care of the new apparatus. This was just the beginning, as it turned out, for it took nearly three months of carrying apparatus home in a potato sack before we ultimately triumphed.

It was not solely his great strength that foiled us for so long but rather his knack for testing each portion of the apparatus to find its weakest point and then focusing all of his attention there. He seemed to go through three distinct phases when presented with a new apparatus: (1) direct strength test which, if unsuccessful, led to (2) exploration of the details, trying to get a foot in the door, as it were, and if that failed, (3) a real strength test! If that failed he lost interest.

During the exploration phase he unscrewed nuts and bolts, and though managing to get the bolt back in the hole from which it was extracted, he didn't succeed in putting the nut back on—but he tried! Pieces of the apparatus were used to pry further pieces off, to pry at the cage door and lock, to hammer bolt heads, gouge at the mortar between concrete blocks in the wall, and then jam the sliding door separating him from the apparatus. Was this the same Bob who couldn't stay interested in objects behind plastic windows long enough to have his intelligence tested?

Fascinated by Bob's strength, we decided to get an objective measure of it. Three long garage door springs were fastened to a handle and stretched out, one at a time, by my hefty assistant Robert Megling, down the inside of a 4-foot section of 7-inch-diameter steel pipe. Although Bob needed no incentive to pull on the handle once he discovered that he could move it, he was rewarded with a bit of fruit each time he pulled more strongly than his last pull. He managed, one-handed, to pull 508 pounds and often 500 pounds four times within one minute—one ton per minute. Big Albert, the silverbacked lowland gorilla, pulled 480 pounds with one hand, but we suspect he was only half trying. Earl Clark, a weight-lifter who won the Mr. Universe and Mr. World titles, could not budge the handle from its resting position, which required a mere 425 pounds of strength.

But Bob's strength is not his greatest asset. He, along with the other two orangutans tested, Roberta and Maggie, were superior manipulators and tool-users as compared to three gorillas and three chimpanzees. They manipulated the object more, and in a greater variety of ways, and paid attention to more of its details than the other two species combined. They also solved the two tool-using problems in less time, and in a more sophisticated manner than the other apes. Bob solved each problem in less than three minutes, including the time spent using the object supplied as a tool to pry at bolt heads and poke into holes, before turning his attention to the problem to be solved.

If we could sum up Bob's personality in a few short phrases, and at the same time characterize the orangutan generally, it would be in Barbara Harrisson's words (paraphrased): A ceaseless curiosity about, and a constant fiddling with, the environment—infinite gentleness in spite of great strength—and a strong capacity to adapt to new conditions. To this we might add: a disdain for monotonous, repetitive tasks. Are these not among the qualities man most admires in himself?

# Oddities in Snakes

## By C.B. Perkins

*C.B. Perkins, known to all as "Si," served as chief herpetologist during the Zoo's formative years and laid the foundation for the present outstanding reptile collection.*

**March 1943**

Snakes are probably the most misunderstood of all animals. There is such a mass of misinformation about them and so many false ideas about their behavior that the real, but peculiar, things that some of them do are generally unknown.

Ranging over most of the United States east of the Rocky Mountains is a small snake that is commonly called hog-nosed snake because its turned-up nose resembles that of a hog. It is a harmless snake and will not even bite, but it has developed a method of self-defense that has given it a bad reputation. When disturbed, the hog-nosed snake puts up what appears to be a terrific fight. It flattens its body and spreads out to about twice its normal size, taking deep breaths and expelling the air with loud hisses. It makes short jabs with its head, but if a stick or finger is placed within reach, the snake "strikes" in another direction. It certainly looks fierce but all this is bluff as it will not bite. If this fails to drive

*Reptile Mesa, Si Perkins' domain, before World War II.*

away the intruder, the snake writhes around and ends up on its back—mouth open and full of dust, tongue hanging out, and to all appearances very dead. It can be picked up, perfectly limp, but gives itself away because if turned over on its belly in normal position it immediately flips over on its back again, apparently believing that a dead snake must be upside down. It not only appears vicious but is often believed to be deadly poisonous, and even its breath is thought to cause sickness and possible death. It is called spreading adder, puff adder, death viper, etc.; all these for a harmless little snake.

The carnivals and similar shows often charge a dime to see THE GREAT HORNED RATTLESNAKE or THE SACRED HORNED RATTLER OF THE SUNWORSHIPERS. It's a fake. A foster spur, a porcupine quill, or a wooden spike has been fastened to the top of the rattler's head. A huge "horn" is usually glued on the top but when a slender "horn" is used it is often forced through the roof of the mouth to stick out the top of the head.

There is a horned rattlenake but its interesting peculiarity is not the horns but its method of locomotion. It is the sidewinder—a small rattler found only on the deserts of the southwestern United States. It has two horns that are merely the enlarged scales above the eye. The usual way in which this snake travels is in the lateral undulating fashion, each part of the body pushing backward against any small resisting substance, such as a bit of grass, a pebble or the loose earth itself. The track left in the sand is a series of disconnected, oblique, parallel lines the length of the snake. The gait reminds one of walking. The snake seems to gallop along and travels faster than any other rattlesnake.

The California boa is a mild tempered snake and does not attempt to bite even when freshly captured. Most specimens crawl through the hands when picked up and some just lie still. Occasionally an individual will roll up in a ball with its head inside the coils, presumably for protection. The giant pythons and boas, to which this little snake is related, have a pelvic girdle with movable spurs in place of hind legs. Only the male California boa has such "legs" and they are so small that they are sometimes overlooked.

It is usually thought that the difference between a snake and a lizard is the possession of legs, but this is not so. Here is a snake with legs, and several species of lizards do not have legs. Most of our lizards have eyelids and ear openings but some do not. A snake has neither. The principal difference between the two is that a lizard has a chin whereas the two lower jaw bones of a snake are not joined together in front with bone.

Several different kinds of snakes vibrate the tail when annoyed, but the habit has reached its peak in the rattlesnakes. Rattlers get a new segment every time they shed, which is several times a year. Too long a string would not be efficient for rattling purposes and parts break off. Seldom does a snake have more than eight or ten segments.

Various reasons have been given to explain why the snake rattles, but the best one seems to be that it can warn any creature that might hurt it. Years ago the ancestors of the bison ranged over a great deal of the country that is inhabited by rattlesnakess.

These great "thundering herds" probably stepped on and killed many snakes and would have been bitten numerous times. The bite undoubtedly was painful but seldom caused death. If the bison associated the noise made by the rattlesnake with the hurt in his leg he quickly would learn to avoid the sound.

Corroborative evidence for this line of reasoning is found in Africa. There on the veldt are the same "thundering herds" and also snakes. In this case, however, evolution arranged a different method whereby the snake could protect itself. Several of these snakes squirt venom a distance of several feet, either in a fine stream or a spray. Their aim at the eye is said to be very accurate. When caring for these "spitting" snakes in captivity, it is necessary to wear goggles. It is true that if the snake becomes angry or nervous and "spits," droplets of venom hit the goggles, but they are also found on the shirt—so maybe their aim isn't as good as usually claimed. At any rate some of the venom would hit the eye of the passing animal and as the mucous membrane of the eye absorbs the poison so rapidly, pain and temporary blindness would be almost instantaneous—and another snake didn't get stepped on.

# Learning To Be a Mother

By Patricia A. Scollay, Ph.D.
Steven Joines
Catherine Baldridge
Americo (Ricky) Cuzzone

*Patricia Scollay was a lecturer in psychology, Steven Joines a student in anthropology and Catherine Baldridge a technical assistant in the college of sciences (all at San Diego State University) when they joined with Americo (Ricky) Cuzzone, a senior keeper at the Wild Animal Park, to teach an unusual course in applied motherhood.*

**April 1975**

Dolly Gorilla was captured in West Africa at the tender age of nine months and spent her most formative years in the skilled and gentle care of humans. She never saw an infant gorilla until, at the age of almost ten years, she gave birth to Jim on October 15, 1973.

He was a strong, healthy infant, weighing six pounds and four ounces, the largest gorilla ever born in captivity. Although Jim was persistent in his attempts to maintain contact with his mother, Dolly was even more adamant in her rejection of him. She repeatedly removed him when he attempted to cling to her. Six hours after birth, Jim was showing signs of being cold and was taken from her cage to the San Diego Wild Animal Park Nursery, where he is being successfully hand-reared.

Almost one year later, on October 2, 1974, Dolly gave birth to a second infant. Binti, a charming little female, has been cared for by her mother since she was born. Dolly has been an exemplary mother and Binti may be one of the few gorillas in captivity to be raised by its mother.

Why has Dolly been such a good mother to Binti after rejecting Jim? One reason may be that Dolly spent the summer between their births in an intensive training program, designed to teach her the fundamentals of motherhood.

Although the Carthaginean explorer Hanno recorded sighting "men of the forest" in the fifth century B.C. and named them gorillas, they were not described for science until 1847. The first gorilla seen alive outside of Africa arrived in London in 1855 and died a few days later. Before the 1930s, few animals were able to withstand the rigors of captivity.

The first viable captive birth occurred in 1956 at the zoo in Columbus, Ohio, and was followed by births at other zoos, including San Diego. Half of the captive births have been in the last four years, but the total is only 105, and roughly 30% of those infants did not survive the first two weeks of life. The poor reproductive record of captive gorillas is particularly unfortunate because of the endangered status of the species. For this reason, it is critical that captive breeding and rearing of these animals be improved.

Western lowland gorillas inhabit the rain forests of equatorial West Africa, spending most of their time on the ground foraging for food. They are exclusively vegetarian, the diet consisting primarily of stalks, vines, bark, and only occasionally fruit. Because this type of food is relatively low in nutritional value, vast quantities must be eaten every day to support an adult male gorilla that typically weighs between three and four hundred pounds (females weigh about half that much).

Gorillas live in relatively permanent groups of from five to thirty. There are usually one or two dominant males called "silverbacks" because of the gray hair in the saddle or lumbar area, and two or three black-backed males that are younger and less dominant, as well as four or five females. The stable group situation allows a young female to choose a male she knows for a mate. Once a female becomes pregnant, she may not engage in sexual behavior again until her youngster is three years old and independent.

Now that some of the problems of diet and health are being solved, breeding has become more frequent in captivity. It may even be more frequent than in the natural environment, due to the fact that most captive-born gorillas are removed from their mothers at birth. This often results in the mother becoming pregnant again within a few weeks, greatly shortening the normal three to four-year birth interval.

This might increase the captive gorilla population but has serious drawbacks because of the severely restricted learning experiences of the captive-born generation. A pessimistic

*Jim, Dolly's first-born, at play poolside.*

*Dolly cuddles her baby Binti.*

but not unrealistic prediction is that few members of this generation will be able to reproduce, or to care for their young if they do reproduce.

There is clearly no strong maternal instinct in higher primates. All evidence suggests that females must learn to care for infants. In some species this is accomplished by allowing juvenile females to share in the care of infants; the young females seem to learn by watching experienced mothers with their babies.

Although young gorillas can most often be hand-raised in good health, this inhibits the development of social skills required for gorillas to interact successfully with other gorillas. The maturing animal has no opportunity to observe adults of its own species.

Gorillas, like humans, have a long developmental period. They spend their first six to eight years learning to do the things many other animals do instinctively: how to care for their future offspring, to use their energy, and to express their emotions in ways that don't disrupt the group. Mature apes that have been raised in a nursery often have difficulty communicating with each other; likewise, their social interactions, aggressive encounters, and even reproductive behaviors are frequently abnormal. It is not surprising, then, that social behavior as complex as maternal care is frequently inadequate.

Maternal behavior can be learned in at least three ways: through experience with an infant, by observation and imitation, and by operant conditioning. When it was determined that Dolly was again pregnant, we attempted to teach her motherhood skills through the use of motion pictures showing gorilla mother-infant care. We soon discovered that movies could not hold Dolly's attention for more than a few seconds. Human children learn that movies, television, and pictures are two-dimensional representations of the real three-dimensional world. Dolly apparently did not learn this and films could not be used to provide her with models for her behavior.

The first weeks of the project were spent gaining Dolly's confidence and trust. Gorillas are shy and gentle animals whose trust is not easily won. Therefore, we relied on their trusted caretaker, Ricky Cuzzone, to make the initial introductions. Dolly became particularly attached to Steve and, as she learned to trust him, he came to know what to expect from her.

Jim was seven months old when the study was begun. Dolly was then between three and four months pregnant. It was possible to bring Jim to the gorilla enclosure for exercise, which gave us an excellent opportunity to reacquaint Dolly with her first offspring. We thought this might serve the dual purpose of giving the infant some much needed experience with an adult gorilla, as well as giving Dolly some experience with an older infant, even though at a distance.

The next and possibly most important phase of the project involved the introduction of a pillow "infant." Made of cream-colored canvas, it roughly approximated the size of an infant without arms or legs. Facial features (simple eyes, nose and mouth) were added with ink. Later in the training program, Steve attempted to give Dolly a more realistic baby, a stuffed toy gorilla. Her reaction to the new toy was a piercing shriek, after which she ran into the next room and refused to come out.

Dolly accepted and played with her pillow doll within five minutes of its first introduction. As she is very responsive to the voice of trusted humans, she was told, in soft reassuring tones, that the doll was a baby and was urged to treat it gently.

Eighty percent of inexperienced gorilla mothers will lick their new infants clean and hold them. However, gorilla mothers need to learn which end of the tiny, squeaking, clinging thing is up and which surface is the front. Thus, one of the commands that Steve taught Dolly was "Turn the baby around, Dolly." If she responded correctly, she was given praise and food reward.

The other commands which Steve taught Dolly were: "Pick up the baby, Dolly"; "Show me the baby, Dolly"; and, "Be nice to the baby, Dolly." Dolly was able to respond correctly to each of these commands within two or three days. By the end of the summer, training sessions were held every day and lasted about three hours, which included long rest periods because Dolly's attention span is relatively short.

At six o'clock on the morning of October 2, Ricky discovered Dolly in labor. Fifteen minutes later the birth was complete. Dolly began caring for Binti immediately. Dolly and Binti remained connected by the umbilical cord for 14 hours before the placenta was delivered. Nursing was first observed 12 hours after birth.

Dolly proved to be an exemplary mother from the first, gently holding Binti close to her body at all times. The first time Binti began to cry, the crying confused Dolly and she did not seem to be able to deal with the situation herself. However, if someone said, "Be nice to the baby, Dolly," she could respond to the command by holding Binti to her chest or abdomen, and in so doing quiet the baby.

Within several weeks, Dolly had learned how to care for Binti when she cried and no longer required a human to prompt her to do the right thing. She continues to be an excellent mother.

# Darwin and the Evolutionary Puzzle

## By Steven Joines

*A century following his death, ZOONOOZ paid its respects to Charles Darwin, the English naturalist whose theories revolutionized the way man looks at himself and his world. Darwin student Steven Joines, who holds a master's degree in physical anthropology, served recently as writer-researcher for "The Animal Express" television series.*

**August 1982**

Charles Darwin laid the cornerstone of modern biological science and revolutionized western thought with his monumental work *The Origin of Species by Means of Natural Selection*. He proposed concretely, for the first time, that species are mutable and explained their mutability through his theory of natural selection. Darwin's arguments favoring the evolutionary development of plants and animals are so persuasive and stimulating that their resulting effects have been felt in every field of academic endeavor. More than a century later, though new views of evolution are advanced, Darwin's theories remain basic to much of our modern research.

Charles Robert Darwin was born on February 12, 1809. His was a prosperous family of liberal scientific background that strongly promoted education and freethinking. His father, the formidable Robert Darwin, who stood more than six feet tall and weighed in excess of 300 pounds, was an active civic leader and a successful physician. Charles was only eight years old when his mother, Suzannah Wedgwood Darwin, daughter of the founder of the renowned Wedgwood pottery works, died.

After his mother's death, Charles was raised by his elder sisters, who, he later acknowledged, instilled within him a spirit of humanity. The intellectual atmosphere in which the Darwin children were reared was due not only to the liberal influence of their Wedgwood relatives, but also to the influence of their paternal grandfather. Erasmus Darwin was a respected physician, who had also gained a reputation as a competent though somewhat eccentric amateur naturalist. Darwin found English public school dull and was an ordinary student by any standards, though he displayed an early interest in chemistry and was an avid collector of natural artifacts. At the age of 16 he enrolled at Edinburgh University to pursue a medical career but remained barely two years because he loathed the study of medicine. In 1828, his father decided that he should be moved to Cambridge, and study to become a clergyman. Charles quickly agreed to this idea, realizing that his future inheritance from his father would be enough to live on comfortably and that the ministry was not so demanding a profession as to interfere with his enthusiasm for natural history or with his avid interest in grouse hunting.

Though he managed to pass his course work at Cambridge, Darwin spent little time pursuing the study of theology. In addition to shooting, he exercised his interests in taxidermy, an art at which he admittedly had little skill, and beetle collecting. Darwin's great fascination for collecting beetles eventually brought him to the attention of the chairman of Cambridge's botany department, John Stevens Henslow.

Darwin and Henslow became fast friends, and the botanist persuaded his disciple to undertake seriously the study of geology. Charles quickly learned the fundamental principles of geology, and his mind was opened to the dynamic nature of the earth.

In addition, Darwin read Baron Alexander von Humboldt's book *A Personal Narrative of Travels to the Equinoctial Regions of America*. Von Humboldt's descriptions of the New World thrilled Darwin, and he began making plans to go to the Canary Islands to see these wonders. Henslow informed him that a Royal Navy captain, Robert Fitzroy, was undertaking a surveying voyage around the world and was looking for someone to accompany him as an unpaid naturalist aboard *H.M.S. Beagle*.

After several meetings with Captain Fitzroy, 22-year-old Charles Darwin, with little

*Darwin's rhea, one of many species named for the famed naturalist.*

H. M. S.
Beagle *in the
Straits of
Magellan.*

formal scientific training, set off on an adventure that was to change his life and ultimately change the world's view of life.

The surveying voyage of *H.M.S. Beagle* lasted from December 27, 1831 until October 2, 1836. The *Beagle's* mission took her to the Cape Verde islands, on to Brazil, down the coast of Argentina to Tierra del Fuego, around Cape Horn, and up the coasts of Chile and Peru to the 15 islands comprising the Galápagos Archipelago, then on across the Pacific to Tahiti, New Zealand, Australia, around the Cape of Good Hope, and finally home.

Nearly five years of exploration and discovery had profoundly altered the character and the beliefs of Charles Darwin. The man who returned to England in the fall of 1836 had become an extraordinarily competent field naturalist whose perceptive abilities, powers of observation, and attention to scientific detail had been finely honed during the voyage. His observations had gradually convinced him that all existing ideas with regard to the fixity of species were invalid. As yet he had not worked out the mechanisms by which species evolve, but his experiences had convinced him that they did.

In the development of the evolutionary thesis, the most important episode for Darwin began on September 15, 1835, when the *Beagle* dropped anchor off Chatham Island in the Galápagos Archipelago, 600 miles west of Ecuador. The Galápagos Archipelago is volcanic in origin, the islands having been thrust above sea level during the late Tertiary period. It is estimated that successful colonization of the islands by animal forms from the South American mainland has taken place only

within the past one million years, following the formation of suitable soils and the successful colonization by plant species.

What impressed Darwin about the fauna of these islands, particularly the birds, was that it bore a clear, yet distant relationship to the fauna forms of South America. In studying the adaptations and distribution of the 13 species of finch which inhabit the Galápagos, Darwin gradually discerned that as a group they formed a microcosm exemplifying the delicate processes of evolutionary development. He noted that while all of the species (now known collectively as Darwin's finches) were closely related, distinct species had arisen to exploit the individual ecological niches available. When compared side-by-side, the beaks of the various finches exhibit gradations in size from small to large.

Some of the finches have small beaks adapted for catching insects or boring in wood, others have beaks suitable for feeding on small seeds and the fruits of various cacti, while others have evolved larger beaks for crushing big seeds with hard shells. Darwin was faced with fundamental questions about species that could not be answered logically by any of the traditionally accepted theories.

During the remaining year of the *Beagle's* voyage, Darwin pondered over the Galápagos finches and the species question in general.

Darwin read Thomas Malthus's *An Essay on the Principle of Population as it Affects the Future Improvement of Society*. Malthus stated that it was impossible to improve humankind's condition because population would always increase in a geometrical ratio (2, 4, 8, 16, 32, 64, 128 . . . ) while food supplies can only increase in an arithmetical ratio. What prevents humans from overpopulating themselves out of existence, Malthus concluded, was that starvation, war, and disease eliminated most people from the gene pool before they had the opportunity to reproduce.

Darwin had found the key he had been searching for to unlock his theory. Malthus had shown him how desperate is the struggle for survival. All species of plants and animals possess awesome reproductive capabilities. What prevents any type of plant or animal from choking the entire planet in a short period of time is that only a minuscule percentage of offspring survive to reproductive maturity. The crux of the matter suddenly became clear; *inter*specific competition for survival, such as that between rattlesnake and kangaroo rat, is not nearly as important as *intra*specific competition for food, living space, and warmth—those essentials to the survival of each individual. The result is that those individuals which possess even the slightest adaptive advantage in this intense competition with members of their own species are the most likely to survive, reproduce, and pass on their advantageous traits.

The transmission of tiny, but nonetheless significant advantages in the struggle for survival, he called natural selection, a simple yet elegant solution to the species question. Relentless intraspecific competition for resources will always favor individuals possessing slightly advantageous variations. Over the course of thousands of generations, the descendants of founding species will incorporate so many inherited favorable variations that collectively they will constitute an entirely new species.

Darwin felt that the best way to present his theory would be in a massive volume which would be too imposing to repudiate. The work of gathering this mountain of evidence in support of his theory was to occupy him for 22 years. However, at the urging of his friends, J.D. Hooker, the botanist, and Sir Charles Lyell, who were worried that his procrastination might cause him to lose his priority, Darwin wrote a brief essay on the subject in 1842 and outlined the theory completely in a 230-page abstract two years later.

On June 18, 1858, it became suddenly apparent that Darwin could no longer indulge himself with procrastination. He received a letter from Alfred Russel Wallace, a 35-year-old naturalist working on the Malay Archipelago. The envelope contained an essay which Wallace had written and sent to Darwin for criticism and circulation among other naturalists. Reading the essay, Darwin was stunned; it covered point by point his own theory of evolution by means of natural selection. In one of those ironic twists of fate, Wallace had chosen Darwin out of all the scientific men in England to be the first to see his essay.

Darwin was faced with an enormous ethical dilemma. Because Wallace had entrusted his essay to him, Darwin felt there was only one honorable course of action. He would relinquish any claims of priority to the theory and publish Wallace's paper on his behalf. Hooker and Lyell dissuaded him in this plan, however, and together devised a solution which gave credit for the discovery to both men equally, yet established Darwin's priority before the scientific community. Lyell and Hooker presented four documents to a meeting of the Linnean Society of London. The first was a letter signed by them explaining the circumstances under which Darwin had received Wallace's essay and that he had intended to publish it on Wallace's behalf but had been convinced otherwise by them in the interest of science. This was followed by excerpts from Darwin's 1844 outline of the theory and a letter dated 1857 showing that Darwin had independently reached all of his conclusions by that year. Finally Wallace's paper was presented to the meeting.

After learning what had transpired in London, Wallace refused to take any credit away from Darwin, pointing out that Darwin had originated the theory many years earlier and had overcome theoretical problems that he, Wallace, had not yet even begun to think about.

Darwin finally realized that if his priority were to be maintained he must, at least, publish his findings. He began work on an abstract of his theory. Working intensely, he managed to complete the manuscript by the end of March 1859. *The Origin of Species by Means of Natural Selection* went on sale on November 24, 1859. The entire edition was sold out within 24 hours and the second edition, released less than two months later, sold equally well.

The general response of theologians was one of vociferous outrage. One of England's leading clergymen proclaimed that Charles Darwin was the most dangerous man in England. Even some of Darwin's teachers and colleagues were hostile. For a time it looked as if Darwin and his theory stood alone.

If older scientists resisted Darwinism because they had built their careers and reputations on other ideologies, this was not the case with their younger colleagues. Evolution had opened up new areas of research, and the new generation of naturalists pursued these opportunities. Scholarly study of the *Origin of Species* continued, and among scientists, the creationist doctrine was soon supplanted by the theory of evolution. Gradually, as the theory spread outside the scientific community, the world began to recognize that the delicate evolutionary forces and interactions described by Darwin were truly wonders of creation.

It was said of Charles Darwin by his scientific colleagues that he had genius, but it was the genius of infinite pains rather than of superhuman intelligence. Darwin's great gift was his ability to formulate generalized laws of science out of huge collections of facts. Charles Darwin died of April 19, 1882 as a result of a heart attack suffered the night before. Although he was never awarded the knighthood usually bestowed upon great scientists (it was rumored that Queen Victoria objected to evolution), he was buried near the tomb of Sir Isaac Newton in Westminster Abbey.

Darwin's influence continued to grow extensively after his death. His significant contributions toward a better understanding of life and the world as it is shared by all living beings have brought Charles Darwin to a level of historical importance accorded only a few great men and women of science.

*(opposite page) Pope's pit vipers (Trimeresurus popeorum)*

*(below) Colorado Desert sidewinder (Crotalus cerastes laterorepens)*

*(above) Flat-tailed day gecko (Phelsuma laticauda). Photo by Susan Schafer.*

*(below) Mexican west coast rattlesnake (Crotalus basiliscus basiliscus)*

7

(upper left)
Emerald tree boa
(Corallus
caninus)

(upper right)
Red-eyed frog
(Agalychnis
callidryas)

(below) Jackson's
chameleon
(Chamaeleo
jacksoni)

# Hey You Up There!

## By Richard Tenaza, Ph.D.

*Upon seeing his first giraffe, one man is reported to have exclaimed, "There ain't no such animal!" While few of us would question the giraffe's existence, most would agree it is a most unusual creature. Richard Tenaza, a University of Pacific Professor, contemplates the giraffe's unique existence.*

**August 1984**

Richard Tenaza

*Male giraffe demonstrated curled lip behavior, a prelude to breeding.*

**M**ost zoo visitors have little to say to or about giraffes. The world's tallest creature is rarely laughed at, waved at, talked to, or jokingly compared to favorite relatives as are many other species.

People seem awestruck by such an enormous, unthreatening being and, despite visual evidence to the contrary, many appear reluctant to believe that the giraffe really exists.

An adult male giraffe standing upright is about 15 feet tall at the top of his horns. By stretching up and extending his tongue, as he does when feeding, a male can reach up to about 18 feet. Females are a foot or two shorter. Being tall gives giraffes of both sexes an advantage over shorter browsers, allowing them to feed from ground level to tree crowns.

Giraffes feed mainly on young, protein-rich leaves of trees and shrubs in the acacia family. They also eat foliage of some broad-leafed plants, and a variety of pods, fruits, twigs, and green thorns.

The giraffe's purplish gray tongue is 16 to 18 inches long. It is a most effective prehensile tool for wrenching leaves and twigs from thorny acacias. Very dry or thorny material eaten by a giraffe is coated with thick, latexlike saliva in the giraffe's mouth, allowing thorns and twigs to be swallowed harmlessly. Tough, horny skin covering the giraffe's palate provides further protection.

In their quest for food, giraffes inadvertently become zealous gardeners, pruning shrubs on the African savannas into domes, cones, hourglasses, and myriad other forms. Like garden hedges, savanna plants respond to pruning by increasing leaf production, which in turn provides more food for giraffes.

Drinking is awkward for giraffes. To reach down to water, a giraffe must spread its forelegs far apart and lower its head. This is as dangerous as it is ungainly, for it leaves the giraffe wide open to attack from lions.

When a giraffe stands upright, its brain is nine feet above its heart, and when it bends to eat or drink at ground level, the brain drops to six feet below the heart. The giraffe is thus faced with the problem of how to prevent rapid, harmful changes in cerebral blood pressure as the head swings up and down. The giraffe's solutions to this problem include a network of elastic arteries at the base of the brain that helps equilibrate pressure; special valves in the jugular vein that pre-

*Giraffes roam free at the Wild Animal Park.*

*A young giraffe receives a maternal licking.*

lions, attacked human hunters, and damaged motorcars with their sledgehammer hooves.

Male giraffes fight among themselves by wrestling with their necks and striking with their horns. Such combat, called necking, usually begins with two foes standing side by side, pushing against one another. Then, one suddenly swings its head and neck over backwards or sideways, attempting to strike the other with its horns. The thud of a heavy blow is audible for 50 to 100 yards. Though appearing to move in slow motion, necking giraffes sometimes strike with enough force to knock out or even kill an opponent. However, most necking involves relatively harmless sparring, between young males. Serious fighting between adult males occurs most often when a female in estrus is nearby. As far as is known, females never fight.

A single young is born after a gestation of 14 to 15 months. The mother stands during parturition, and the calf drops rudely into the world from six feet up. A calf can stand within 5 minutes and begins suckling in 20 to 45 minutes. Giraffes mature at 3 to 4 years and have lived as long as 28 years in captivity.

Giraffes less than six months old are often grouped in a crèche. A crèche forms when several mothers leave their calves together in a conspicuous, open place while they go off foraging, perhaps a mile or more away. Typically, a mother visits the crèche in early morning and late evening to nurse her calf. The young may be left alone, or the crèche may be guarded by one or more adults.

A moderately fast-walking giraffe uses a gait called the pace, in which both limbs on the same side swing together. When the giraffe speeds up to a run, its gait changes to one in which both forelimbs and both hind limbs move together. Speeds up to 35 miles per hour are attained, with the front legs providing the main power.

One might anticipate that creatures so large and so mobile would be great wanderers. The majority are not. In most regions, the area used by the giraffe during the year varies from a minimum of three to a maximum of only thirty square miles.

British zoologist Desmond Morris found that the giraffe is among the top ten favorite animals in England. He attributed the giraffe's popularity to its erect, humanlike posture, which causes us to view it as a stretched-out caricature of ourselves.

The giraffe evokes another, almost supernatural, sensation. A giraffe's presence can fire an emotional experience comparable to that felt upon entering a great Gothic cathedral or standing beneath a giant California sequoia. It stirs awareness of how small we are in the vastness of nature.

vent a backflow of blood to the brain when the giraffe bends down; and a mechanism that automatically decreases heart rate and central arterial blood pressure when the giraffe lowers its head.

Lions and humans are the giraffe's most dangerous enemies. Cheetahs and leopards take an occasional calf, and crocodiles may capture an unwary adult, but these are rare events. Large eyes and a watchtower neck enable the giraffe to spot danger from afar. Its ability to sight distant predators makes the giraffe a valued member of the herbivore community; when a giraffe stretches up and stares out over the plains, shorter animals stop what they are doing to look, listen, and sniff the air for danger.

Giraffes usually run from predators. However, if surprised or cornered, a giraffe defends itself or its calf by kicking outward with its forefeet. Wild giraffes have killed

# Dragons Big and Bold

## By Charles E. Shaw

*Dragons are generally found only in old fairy tales or their modern equivalent, the science-fiction film. But there is one real-life dragon which roams the earth, or at least a small corner of it, as Charles E. Shaw, then curator of reptiles, reveals.*

**October 1963**

*A pair of dragons enjoy the sun at the Zoo.*

"**C**rates measure 86 inches by 29 inches by 23 inches. Gross weight 280 Kilos. Arrive Los Angeles August 13, 9:00 P.M., Flight 818 Pan American."

So read the terse cable announcing the arrival of a pair of Komodo dragons.

The world's largest and probably most zealously protected lizard, the Komodo dragon occurs in a rather restricted area of Indonesia almost directly east of Java: the islands of Komodo, Rintja, Padar, and a narrow strip of the west coast of Flores.

Legal acquisition may be had only with the sanction of the Indonesian Government, which rarely issues permits for their capture. Unfortunately some poaching occurs, as black market specimens occasionally are offered at exorbitant prices by unscrupulous smugglers.

The Komodo dragon is a member of the monitor family of lizards which includes about 30 species. The group is a venerable one with an ancestry dating back some sixty million years. Today, the monitor lizards are confined to the old world in Africa, Asia and Australia. Some of these reach a size no larger than eight to ten inches, while others are a respectable five to six feet in length.

The Komodo dragon, however, is the giant of the family, attaining a length of about ten feet and a weight of nearly 300 pounds in the males. Females are somewhat shorter in length and not so heavy.

Like the other members of its family, the Komodo dragon is strictly carnivorous, feeding on whatever may become available to it, including carrion, but to say the Komodo dragon lives predominately on carrion, as has been claimed, is to presume a good deal more carrion than seems possible in the comparatively restricted area in which these lizards are found.

The Komodo monitor has keen eyesight, reacting immediately to the slightest movement of possible prey. It would seem likely that the majority of food items devoured

*The head of the dragon.*

actually are run down and killed before being eaten. Deer, boar and water buffalo, as well as other smaller mammals, birds and their eggs, fish, and other reptiles, perhaps even including the Komodo's own eggs and young, are eaten by the giants.

The natives living in the same areas where the dragons are found refer to them as "buaya darat," or land crocodile, a name that seems entirely appropriate in view of the beasts' size and voracious food habits.

As if deliberately exiled by nature, the dragon inhabits one of the driest regions of the Indonesian Archipelago. Rainfall there is scant, briefly turning to green the alangalang grass covering the Lontar palm-dotted hills and valleys. During the major part of the year the sere landscape bears only small,

*The world's largest and most ferocious lizard.*

scattered mud or water holes, where various animals come to drink. In these surroundings the Komodo dragon spends its life, foraging for food by day and retiring into natural or self-made dens beneath rocks or tree trunks for the night.

Since the native animals are so important to the continued existence of the giant lizard, hunting of any kind is prohibited on the islands of Rintja and Padar, where a dragon reserve has been established. This measure together with the protection of wild game on Komodo Island, where hunting is a privilege reserved only for the permanent inhabitants, assures that the Komodo dragon now is reasonably safe from the competition and exploitation of its chief enemy—Man!

# Discovering Treasures of China

## By Marjorie Betts Shaw

*In China there exist forms of wildlife found nowhere else and unknown to the western world until their discovery a century ago by an adventurous Catholic missionary. ZOONOOZ editor Marjorie Shaw reports on this unique man's life and accomplishments.*

**November 1984**

High in the land of the clouds live jeweled birds of silver and gold, fire foxes, sure-footed beasts that wear the golden fleece, and monkeys of gold and aquamarine with capes of gilded silk. Once in the land of clouds, in order to see many of these creatures of fable and myth, one must travel to the Land of the Western Barbarians.

In 1862, Jean Pierre Armand David, a Catholic priest, was sent to the Lazarist mission in Peking. The 36-year-old cleric had a strong foundation in natural history and was to discover for science much of the legendary wild fauna and flora of China.

Sichuan, known to the Chinese as the land of the clouds, is abundantly rich in wildlife, harboring one-quarter of China's animals, many of them rarities. The Hsifan mountains in the "barbarous west" of Sichuan province lie on the frontier between China and Tibet and are particularly rich in wild species. The steep mountains provide habitat for animals at home in subtropical environments and for those that prefer alpine meadows.

Pére David began his explorations of this rugged landscape only 20 years after China was opened to Europeans. He remained in China for 12 years collecting natural history specimens for the museum of natural history in Paris. Although he was primarily interested in ornithology, his collecting efforts extended to all disciplines.

Perhaps the missionary's most famous discovery was the giant panda, but in Muping he found an animal which had been depicted in Chinese art for several centuries, often as a demon, and which looked so odd it had been presumed a product of the imagination. Pére David recorded his discovery of the legendary animal on May 4, 1869:

My hunters, who left a fortnight ago for the eastern regions, return today and bring me six monkeys of a new species which the Chinese call *chin-tsin-hou*, or golden-brown monkey. The animals are very robust and have large, muscular limbs. Their faces are very

*Golden pheasant.*

strange, green-blue or turquoise with the nose turned up almost to the forehead. Their tails are long and strong. Their backs are covered with long hair and they live in trees in the highest mountains, now white with snow.

The Western world was about to discover the snow monkey, golden monkey, gold silk monkey, snub-nosed monkey, eventually Roxellana's monkey; but though discovered, it would remain largely unknown outside China for another century.

Throughout Pére David's diaries are scattered references to his relentless search for the elusive Chinese monal.

He did eventually obtain specimens of what he called, "this splendid, this superb, this royal game," and, in Muping, captured a living Chinese monal which went to the zoological garden in Paris.

On his third expedition, Pére David fell ill and retired to Europe in 1874. He never returned to China, but spent his remaining 26 years in Paris, devoting the majority of his time to the scientific study of his collections and to teaching.

His two-volume work *Les Oiseaux de la Chine*, published in 1877, recorded 772 birds he had seen, roughly 60 of which had not previously been described. He also identified 200 mammalian species, 63 of them new to science. Through his collections, Pére David gave many new plants to the Western world—among them 52 new species of rhododendron, 3 magnolias, 4 firs, 4 oaks, and several roses.

It was a full and fascinating life for this Basque youth who had traveled to the land of the clouds and gazed upon an extravagance of wildlife—many striking pheasants, jeweled birds of silver and gold; lesser pandas, or fire foxes; and takins, resplendent in their golden fleece. He died in Paris on November 10, 1900. His rarest discoveries, and those for which he is probably best remembered, are undoubtedly the giant panda, and the monkey of gold and aquamarine, with a cape of gilded silk—the golden monkey.

*Temminck's tragopan. Photo by David Rimlinger (upper left)*

*Goral. (upper right)*

*Lesser panda. (lower)*

*Giant panda.*

# Those Odd Hornbills

## By K. C. Lint

*What do the hornbill and the elephant have in common? Both are sources of ivory. K. C. Lint, curator of birds emeritus, reveals that this isn't the only unusual feature of the hornbill, varieties of which are found throughout Africa and Southeast Asia.*

**January 1972**

There are many strange and wonderful forms in the bird world, but none attracts as much attention when first seen by zoo visitors as the group known as hornbills. They are large in size, grotesque in appearance, and most of them have strange nesting habits. Following the selection of a hollow tree by a pair, the male will partially seal the cavity with mud to imprison the female. During the incubation and brooding periods he will feed his mate through a slit opening.

Trademarks of the hornbill family are the bill and casque which may be large or small, curved or straight, smooth or serrated, according to the species. Ornamental casques, or helmets, cover the head and the base of the bill in many of the forms. Each bill and casque is colorful, patterned in white, ivory, black, brown, red or yellow.

Nature's purpose in providing such a bill is still a mystery to naturalists. It has been suggested that because of its strength and weight, it is used to excavate holes in trees for nesting

*Hornbill ivory carving.*

*Concave-casqued hornbill.*

*The carving of hornbill ivory has been practiced as an art form for centuries by the Chinese.*

cavities. Again, it serves as a mason's trowel for applying plaster to the nesting hole.

Hornbills are omnivorous, eating both plant and animal food. In captivity they will eat almost anything. They will accept budget-priced items such as sweetened bread and milk, boiled rice, and kibbled dog food with karo syrup. This somewhat lessens the cost of satisfying their terrific appetites. More costly fruits, berries, small rodents, and eggs may be fed occasionally as supplements.

The hornbill's only difficulty in captivity is defective feather growth. On a large country estate, a ranch, and in a garden some of these forms could be given their liberty with little fear of straying. They do make tame and affectionate pets, but most individuals need a cage or aviary to match the bird's size. They enjoy being petted and handled by adults. In a favorable environment, some will follow an owner about like a dog and command attention.

For centuries the carving of hornbill ivory has been an oriental art performed by the finest craftsmen and many examples are of museum quality. Only the Helmeted hornbill boasts a solid casque, epithema, or excrescence, which may be carved.

Hornbill ivory, the solid yellow substance of the helmet covered at the top and sides by a strong sheath of shiny, brilliant red, is highly prized for carving into art objects such as earrings, belt buckles and snuff bottles. The Chinese refer to it as "ho-ting," their attempt at reproducing the word "gading," Malay for ivory. It is also used for carvings of finger rings, bracelets, spoons, plume holders, and many other small articles.

In addition, the entire skull is variously carved and prized as an object of art. Favorite subjects are religious symbols and figures, events in history and rebuses, such as "May everything turn out as you wish." There are dragons, Fo dogs or lions, and horses, as well as scenes symbolizing long life, joy and happiness.

*Rhinoceros hornbill.*

*Buton hornbill.*

# Bipes, the Elusive Two-Legged Lizard

## By Charles E. Shaw

*Former curator of reptiles Chuck Shaw, together with most herpetologists, believed acquiring an ajolote almost an impossibility—until he asked Hope Warren to look for it. Shaw got both the rare lizard and its ingenious captor; he and Hope were later married.*

**August 1962**

"Amphisbaena, L. (Gr. amphisbaina), a fabulous serpent having a head at each end; now applied to a genus of lizards." So goes the dictionary definition. But what the categorization fails to take into account is an even more incredible, seemingly double-ended saurian that has legs only at one end!

The amphisbaenids number approximately 150 species concerning which there is yet some controversy. Are they really lizards? Or, are they a separate order of reptiles to be ranked with the lizards, snakes, turtles, crocodilians and tuatara? Are they, possibly, not even reptiles?

Certainly, these "lizards," as we shall call them for the time being, should arouse the curiosity of more than a few zoologists and anatomists. Subterranean burrowers, the amphisbaenids not only appear as exaggerated earthworms, but behave in a somewhat similar manner when crawling about on the surface of the ground. Their long, cylindrical bodies ringed with whorls of small scales separated by grooves, their shielded eyes lying beneath the skin, their lack of external ears, and the usual absence of limbs, lend these lizards a most wormlike appearance. To further this deception, the head and tail are generally bluntly similar in appearance. One of the methods of locomotion, that of hitching forward, is most wormlike. These traits, taken in combination with their subterranean mode of life, have earned these intriguing creatures the name "worm" lizards.

Mainly tropical in distribution, approximately half the species of worm lizards are found in the Western Hemisphere. The remaining forms occur principally in Africa, while a single species is found in Spain and three other live in southwestern Asia. The Florida Worm Lizard of northeastern and central Florida is the only amphisbaenid occuring in the United States. The majority of worm lizards are about a foot in length; and the giant of the family, hailing from central Africa, measures a mere 27 inches over all.

Though most worm lizards have simple, blunt heads, a few have developed sharpened, shovel-shaped snouts (some in a horizontal plane, others in a vertical plane), presumably to increase their digging efficiency in hard-packed soil.

Ants, termites, and other small invertebrates probably are the sole diet of worm lizards. The worm lizards are allegedly immune to the bites and stings of soldier ants and termites, a decided advantage to reptiles whose lives are dependent upon such food sources.

Little is known of the life history of most species. A few are known to rely on termitaries not only as a principal source of sustenance, but also as places for the deposition of their eggs—a larder as well as an incubator, and all under the same roof! Only a single African species so far is known to bear living young.

All three species of the genus *Bipes* (two feet) are natives of western Mexico. Two species occur in the Mexican state of Guerrero, while the third is found as close to home as the southern portion of Baja California.

Thomas H. Streets, M.D., was responsible for obtaining the first worm lizard from Baja California. Dr. Streets was surgeon on board the *U.S.S. Narragansett* during the period 1874-1875 while the ship was engaged in a

*Hope Warren Shaw and her prize catch.*

*Closeup of the ajolote, showing its small front legs.*

survey of the coasts of the peninsula. Dr. Streets noted that "the Mexican name for this reptile is *ajolote*. I was informed that it lives mostly underground, coming out only at night. Its rudimentary eyes and the arrangement and shape of the feet, which are similar to those of the mole, would suggest subterrestrial habits, as would also the absence of coloring matter in its integument."

In the nearly ninety years that have passed since the collection of Dr. Streets' specimen, the ajolote or Belding's Mole Lizard, as it is sometimes called, has remained one of the rarest reptiles of the western hemisphere, if not the world. Probably less than three dozen individuals have reached museum collections.

Recently, Miss Hope Warren of the Public Affairs Department, KOGO-TV, Channel 10 in San Diego, visited La Paz, Baja California. Miss Warren asked us what we would like to have in the reptile line from the La Paz area. Jokingly we suggested that a few two-legged worm lizards would be very desirable additions to our collections. We also assured her that chances of acquiring them were just about nil, based on the experience of previous collectors in the area. However, we failed to reckon with Miss Warren's background in the field of mass communication.

Reaching La Paz, Miss Warren immediately started the "ajolote campaign" by presenting herself at Radio Station XENT, and contracting for three twenty-second spot announcements daily for a four-day period. A financial reward was offered to any collector who showed up with ajolotes. A novel collecting technique, indeed!

The first day brought no results. On the evening of the second day, an elderly Mexican appeared with two adult ajolotes. The following evening a small boy brought in four more. Success beyond the wildest dreams! Worm lizards became almost as common as dirt with the acquisition of five more, for a total of eleven. Like many "rare" animals, the ajolote probably is not a really uncommon creature at all—it's all in knowing where to look!

The unique little lizards, the longest of which measured nine inches, were placed in an aquarium with about two inches of fine beach sand. Water was poured into one end of the aquarium to provide a moisture gradient so that the lizards might select the conditions most to their liking.

They made themselves quite at home and constructed permanent, open burrows in the damper sand. During the day the lizards are seldom visible. But at night, one or more frequently can be seen wandering about over the sand surface.

On hard-packed land, or on a smooth, unyielding surface, the front end of the ajolote may progress in a normal, lizard fashion. The remainder of the body is handled in one or both of two ways. Employing a method of serpentine locomotion, the two-legged lizards use the "hitch forward—pull up" or "concertina" method of movement. It is not unusual for the lizard to crawl in a horizontal, undulatory type of locomotion, with loops of the body thrown from side to side in typical snake fashion.

Burrowing in loose, unpacked sand is accomplished by folding the diminutive legs against the body and twisting the head from side to side in an almost circular motion. On hard-packed soil the extremely well-developed, mole-like claws are brought into play and are used for digging simultaneously with the thrust and twist of the body and head.

# The Quagga Commemorated

## By James M. Dolan, Jr., Ph.D.

*Once the quagga roamed South Africa's plains by the thousands. Today it is gone, another casualty in man's thoughtless use of nature. Dr. James Dolan, general curator of mammals, recalls this extinct and almost forgotten creature.*

**August 1983**

On the 12th of August 1883, alone in her stall at the Amsterdam Zoo, a quagga mare (*Equus quagga*) breathed her last, and with her demise an entire race of living creatures crossed the threshold into oblivion, an example of cupidity and waste at the hands of man.

At the time of European settlement of South Africa, the quagga was an abundant equine although it was restricted to the central plains of the Cape Colony and the veldt of the Orange Free State.

Early travelers in South Africa attest that the quagga was abundant on the open plains. John Barrow, Secretary to the Admiralty, who traveled in South Africa in 1797, wrote that the hills that surrounded the plains of Geel-bek were composed of a dark purple-colored slate; and among these were seen a great number of species of wild horse, known in the colony by the Hottentot name *qua-cha*.

Cornwallis Harris, in a book dealing with his famous expedition in the year 1836-37, describes the quagga as follows: "Moving slowly across the profile of the oceanlike horizon, uttering a shrill barking neigh, of which its name forms a correct imitation, long files of quaggas continually remind the early traveler of a river caravan on its march."

Burchell, in 1812, found them in troops of 30 to 50 on the plains. These made a most im-

*This female in the London Zoo was the only quagga to be photographed while still living.*

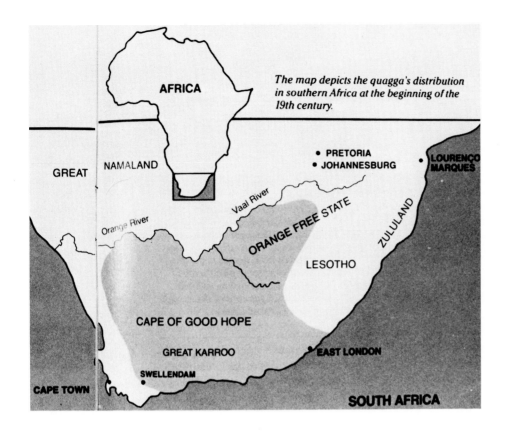

The map depicts the quagga's distribution in southern Africa at the beginning of the 19th century.

*The quagga's range at the beginning of the 19th century.*

pressive sight traveling in single file as was their habit, or when disturbed, wheeling in unison like a squad of cavalry.

The frontier Boers of the Cape Colony fed their Hottentots and other servants on the meat of the quagga and the white-tailed gnu. The Boers took a heavy toll on them in these years, seriously reducing their numbers so that by the late 1850s the quagga was all but extinct south of the Orange River. In the Great Karroo, where they once roamed in tens of thousands, they were certainly gone by 1860.

About 1865, the Boers of the Orange Free State began exploiting the large game animals for their hides. With characteristic industry and deadly skill, skins were gathered and shipped to the coast by the wagonload; hides of the quagga and Burchell's zebra were in particular demand. Quagga hides were also used for grain sacks, and in 1876 during Bryden's visit to South Africa he was shown old quagga-hide sacks which were used to carry dried fruits and nuts. These sacks were of considerable antiquity as the quagga was already extinct in the Cape Colony.

The exact date of extermination of the quagga in the wild is unknown, but it is generally believed that the species survived in the Orange Free State until 1878.

Quaggas had been exported to Europe as early as the late part of the 18th century. Possibly the first animal to reach Europe was a specimen in the collection of the Prince of Wales.

Another early animal was a stallion kept at Versailles by King Louis XVI. Its remains are preserved in the Museum National d'Histoire Naturelle, Paris. Early in the 19th century Mr. Parkins, a sheriff of the City of London, drove a phaeton through Hyde Park, London, drawn by a pair of quaggas. Quaggas were also imported into the United States and were represented in circuses and traveling menageries during the early and mid-19th century.

A female was received in the Berlin Zoo in 1863 and lived until 1867. The London Zoo received three quaggas. The first, a stallion, lived until 1834. His skin is mounted in the British Museum. The second London animal was a mare that lived until 1872. Her skeleton is now housed at Yale University, and her skin at the Royal Scottish Museum, Edinburgh. She is a particularly famous animal as she is the only quagga known to have been photographed in life. London's final quagga was a stallion which lived until 1864. His skeleton is housed in the British Museum, and his skin is preserved in the Natural History Museum at Wiesbaden, West Germany.

The most famous of all quaggas was the last known living specimen. This mare, received at the Amsterdam Zoo on May 9, 1867, died quietly on August 12, 1883, long after the last of her race had sent its barking cry across the plains of South Africa.

# The Quagga is Gone But its Genes May Survive

## By Oliver Ryder, Ph.D.

*Bringing an extinct species, such as the quagga, back to life through retrieval of its genetic material seems far beyond science's capability but Zoo geneticist Dr. Oliver Ryder speculates on what the future may hold.*

**August 1983**

Our current understanding of the evolutionary relationships between animal species, and their scientific classification, has been largely derived from studies of comparative morphology. For large mammals, studies of skin and skeletal specimens predominate.

Over the last several decades additional techniques have become available, based on comparisons of molecules rather than skins, skulls, and other bones. Some of the molecules used for comparison are proteins, for example, albumin or hemoglobin from the blood. Other workers have focused on the DNA (deoxyribonucleic acid) molecules that encode the genetic information of an organism.

Because DNA is the physical code for heritable traits, comparison of DNA molecules has provided solutions to some enigmas left unresolved by traditional methods.

Under normal circumstances, fresh or freshly frozen blood or other tissue is required for molecular evolutionary studies. It has, however, been possible to analyze blood types in preserved Egyptian mummies and to study blood proteins from the tissues of extinct mammoths preserved frozen.

When Reinhold Rau, a noted quagga expert, informed me that he had discovered some vascular and even fleshy tissue while remounting a 150-year-old quagga specimen for the Mainz Natural History Museum in West Germany, the idea of performing molecular studies on the quagga gained feasibility. The fact that the skin was so old suggested that modern tanning techniques (which make most molecular studies impossible) were not used. Preliminary studies suggested that protein could be obtained from the quagga skin specimens.

Shortly after these encouraging findings, we were fortunate to collaborate with a team from the University of California, Berkeley. A fragment of skin provided by Reinhold Rau from the Mainz quagga was treated with detergents and enzymes in order to release DNA much in the same fashion as a fresh tissue sample is treated for DNA extraction.

*Mounted quagga (pictured alive in preceding article) now resides in the Royal Scottish Museum warehouse.*

Oliver Ryder

(The genetic information encoded in an organism's genes is specified by the pattern of bases making up the DNA molecules. Thus, isolating DNA from an extinct quagga is tantamount to isolating the genes of an extinct animal.)

But was the DNA isolated by the Berkeley team really quagga DNA, or was it from bacteria present on the old skin? The DNA was sized and tested for its similarity to the DNA of a living species of zebra, the Hartmann's Mountain zebra. The results were clear. The DNA extracted from the 150-year-old quagga skin contained DNA like that of living zebras. This material contained quagga genes! Little of the material was obtained, however. The quantities of the extracted DNA used in the preliminary experiments are measured in nanograms (billionths of a gram).

In order to study these very rare pieces of DNA, the techniques of recombinant DNA research will be employed so that we may preserve and amplify the quagga DNA sequences. We cannot be sure at this time that the first efforts to clone quagga genes will be successful because of technical considerations.

It is exciting, nonetheless, to consider that although the quagga disappeared from the Great Karroo more than 100 years ago, we may still be able to learn additional aspects of its biology.

# The Fabled Golden Monkey

## By Marjorie Betts Shaw

*San Diego and zoos in the People's Republic of China have developed a close and cordial relationship, resulting in the acquisition of several species seldom seen in the west, including—as ZOONOOZ editor Marjorie Shaw describes—the rare and beautiful golden monkey.*

**December 1984**

*Roxelana, for whom the golden monkey is named.*

Reha Gunay, Topkapi Museum, Istanbul

From its earliest representation, it seems that the golden monkey had its reality based in myth, art, and literature rather than in fact. Despite its discovery in 1869, until recently there has been little but legend surrounding the golden monkey. Even the story of the sultana for whom *Rhinopithecus roxellanae* was named reads like a fairy tale.

She was a slave who captivated a sultan. More than four centuries later, her story captured the imagination of a French zoologist. Turkish raiders had abducted a Russian girl in Galicia, then a province of east central Europe. Her engaging and infectious wit caused them to call her Khurrem, the Laughing One. She became a sultan's prize and entered the harem of Suleiman the Magnificent in 1523.

Seldom have harem women so influenced history that they would be remembered centuries later. However, Roxelana, as she came to be called (a corruption of Russolana, referring to her Russian heritage), held the sultan in thrall and wielded great power. She was his confidante and became his wife—an astounding feat, for Turkish sultans had not married for several hundred years. First as courtesan and companion, then as wife and mother, Roxelana held Suleiman's devotion for half his lifetime. Upon her death, he erected a mosque in the name of Khasseki Khurrem, the Favored Laughing One.

Though her ability to inspire fidelity and to wield power and her enchanting wit may have drawn the attention of Alphonse Milne-Edwards some 400 years later, it was her appearance that caused him to celebrate her by giving her name to a spectacular-looking new primate.

She was described as having a face that showed intelligence and pride, with high cheekbones, a fine, pointed chin, immense, clear eyes of an intense blue, a small mouth with full lips drawn in the form of a heart, and a smile at the same time candid and perverse, which gave her a singular, very alluring expression.

The characteristic that must have immediately come to mind, however, was her blonde and silky hair, with reflections of russet gold, which trailed over her back, down to her ankles. Here, indeed, was a trait shared by the silken-tressed, golden-hued monkey sent by Pére Armand David to Milne-Edwards at the Paris Museum of Natural History.

Zoologists suddenly became interested in the entity which had previously intrigued only scholars. The monkey demon with the turquoise face, red and gold body, and a nose turned up to its eyes, as depicted in ancient Chinese art and fables, really existed, although parts of the early description remained fanciful.

At the beginning of the 12th century A.D., an illustrated book of odes appeared with block prints of fauna and flora of ancient China, reputedly based on paintings from the 4th century. It mentions the *wei* with an upturned nose and long tail.

Kuo P'o, a scholar who lived from 276–324 A.D., comments, "The *wei* resembles the macaque but is larger. Its color is yellowish black, its tail several feet long, resembling an otter's tail, forked at the tip. Its nostrils are tilted upward; when it rains the *wei* hangs

金絲猴

*Golden monkey
(Rhinopithecus
roxellanae).
Watercolor by
Bill Noonan,
the Zoo's
graphic
designer.*

*The golden monkey, creature of Chinese folklore.*

from a tree and covers its nostrils with its tail, or with two fingers.''

In much of Chinese culture the monkey symbolizes ugliness and trickery, and is thought to control goblins, witches, and other denizens of the netherworld. Therefore, it is often worshipped for its ability to prevent sickness and poverty.

The gold-silk monkey was admired for its beauty but has also been hunted for its hair, bones, and meat for nearly 1,000 years. The meat was considered a source of strength, and the bones (when soaked in wine or boiled into jelly) were used as medicine to relieve arthritis and heart trouble. During the Ch'ing Dynasty, the skins of golden monkeys were made into capes to be worn only by the Manchu officials. Such garments were expected to ward off rheumatism.

Today, the monkeys are viewed collectively as a national treasure, depicted on scrolls and stamps and wildlife posters. The monkeys enjoy government protection and there are strict regulations against shooting and capture. Three subspecies exist, and *Rhinopithecus roxellanae roxellanae* has by far the largest population, estimated at 10,000 to 13,000. *Rhinopithecus roxellanae bieti* occurs in a limited area, has long been hunted, and has a small population of about 500. *R. r. brelichi* is the most endangered, with a population of only 200 individuals.

Golden monkeys are large and robust, males weighing about 30 pounds, females 10

pounds less. They stand two to three feet high, with capes that trail from their shoulders, sometimes to a length of 18 or more inches. Their tails measure 20 to 28 inches, but are not forked, as legend would have it. They share their high mountain home with the takin, a variety of pheasant, the musk deer, Tibetan black bear, serow, and lesser and giant pandas.

Golden monkeys of the *roxellanae* subspecies occur in surprisingly large troops of 20 to 30 and sometimes 300 to 600 individuals. They exhibit a practical method of enduring the cold in their snow-covered mountains. They hug each other—for long periods. Faces are buried in their silky fur and the long tails twine about the package securely. When a female feels the need for a warm, masculine hug, she nudges her partner with the top of her head. She always initiates; he always responds.

Although the golden monkey is protected, it is still illegally hunted from time to time. More recently, in some areas of its range, it has been shot as a hairy wild man, or *yeren*. Old legends die hard. Lately the stories seem to be growing. More than 100 hairs from supposed wild men have been collected. Primatologist Frank Poirier examined some of the hair, which was long, gold and russet, and found it to match exactly the shoulder hair of the golden monkey.

# Animals of the Bible

## By M. Eskolsky

*Animals appear frequently in the Scriptures—but have they suffered in translation? M. Eskolsky of the Jerusalem Biblical Zoo suggests that they have and makes an attempt to clear up the confusion over which animals the Bible's authors were actually talking about.*

**December 1954**

All of us know the story of the first zoo—the Bible tale of the flood and the Ark aboard which Noah took a pair of specimens of "every beast after his kind, and all the cattle after their kind, and every creeping thing that creepeth upon the earth after his kind, and every fowl after his kind, every bird of every sort" (Genesis VII:14), thus ensuring an eternal supply of exhibits for zoos. Except for this story, and perhaps the episode of Jonah and the whale, few of us think of animals in connection with the Bible. If we do, we are likely to remember the domesticated camel and donkey, both so frequently mentioned in Scriptures and both so common in the Middle East lands where the events recorded in the Bible occurred. Or perhaps we think of the lion that King David slew as a young shepherd.

Yet scattered throughout the Bible are hundreds of references to animals, birds, reptiles, fish, insects, sometimes merely casually mentioned but sometimes specifically described.

The authors of the Bible knew what they were writing about. They lived in rural communities. Even their cities, like many cities in the Middle East today, were more intimately linked with country life than are modern American and European cities. They lived close to nature. Some of them were farmers. Others were shepherds. Some were fishermen. Throughout the ages, farmers and shepherds and fishermen and others whose livelihood depends on nature have known and studied the wildlife about them.

It was therefore only natural for these men, when they composed their immortal prophecies and poetry and parables, to have frequent recourse to the vivid events in the world of nature, events that were impressed on their imaginations from early childhood. "Go to the ant, thou sluggard," said King Solomon (Proverbs VI: 6). He was teaching a nation in which every man, woman and child saw ants every day and observed their habits. He himself, as a young prince in King David's palace, lived in comparative splendor; but

Jerusalem was then a tiny town, practically a village. The streets were unpaved; the fields were near; every house had a garden; and one may imagine young Solomon must have spent many fascinating hours lying on the ground and watching the ant colonies. Years later, when he needed a model of diligent industry, he turned almost instinctively to the ant.

However, the zoological terminology of the Bible as we know it today suffers from a serious drawback. The men who wrote the Bible knew the world of nature. The men who translated the Bible from the original Hebrew, Aramaic, and Greek were great scholars and sensitive stylists with an unmatched gift of expression; but most of them knew little about natural history, and even less about the wildlife of the Holy Land and the Middle East. They therefore had to draw often on the contexts of the verses in which animals appeared, making intelligent guesses.

If you read your Bible, you will not meet the hedgehog. The Hebrew word "kipod" occurs in Isaiah XIV:23 and XXIV:11, and in Zephaniah II:14. All three times it is rendered in English as "bittern." Yet the word "kipod" has been in unbroken use in Hebrew for thousands of years, and it has always meant hedgehog, the "long-eared desert hedgehog" which is so common in Israel's fields to this very day. The error of the translators in rendering it as "bittern" is typical of a number of such mistakes.

Another example is the famous verse, "The voice of the turtle is heard in our land" (Song of Songs II:12). On the face of it, this verse makes little sense. The turtle is a voiceless creature. Moreover, the original Hebrew "tor" is used a great many times elsewhere in the Bible, always clearly referring to a dove. The bird in question is often named turtledove. Was it perhaps the "palm dove" still to be found in Israel?

For centuries scholars have been trying to clear up these and similar questions. When an animal is mentioned more than once in the Bible, so that it is possible to "cross-index" it and deduce its probable identity, or when a word is so common that its exact meaning is inescapable, or when the context makes it clear what animal is meant by a certain word, the task has not been too hard.

But what about a word which is mentioned only once, with few, if any, clues? For example, the Hebrew "s'mamith" (Proverbs XXX:28), usually translated as "spider." The Authorized Version gives: "The spider taketh hold with her hands, and is in kings' palaces." This is the only mention of "s'mamith" in Scriptures. The word has for many centuries been out of common use. Does the context of the verse "taketh hold with her hands" remind the reader of a spider?

Some commentaries feel the animal in question was a species of lizard, which has more "hand-like" hands than a spider, and is often to be seen in Israel darting across the sunny stone walls, which would probably exist in an ancient king's palace.

Then there are the mythical animals—the unicorn, the dragon, the leviathan. These animals never existed. Did the authors of the Bible believe in their existence? Are these words mistranslations of names of real animals? Or did the authors of the Bible merely use them in a poetic sense, aware all along that they were imaginary creatures?

There is one zoo that makes a specialty of exhibiting the animals and birds mentioned in the Bible—the Jerusalem Biblical Zoo. Here many animals and birds which were once part of the landscape of the Holy Land, but which vanished in the course of centuries, have been collected and are exhibited. On their cages and other enclosures are plaques inscribed with verses from the Scriptures, in Hebrew and in English, mentioning or describing the animals or birds inside.

The Jerusalem Biblical Zoo is set in a lovely natural park, on a hillside thickly wooded with many of the trees mentioned in the Bible and studded with rock formations. The paths are unpaved, and wind around trees instead of leading across places where trees used to be. Fencing is unobstrusive and inconspicuous. The visitor sees a picturesque panorama in which animals roam in the same mountainous setting in which they lived thousands of years ago—and as the authors of the Bible saw them.

# I Never Saw a Purple Cow . . .or a shovel-headed tree frog, either!

## By Carole Towne
## Drawings By Bill Noonan

*Public relations director Carole Towne speculated on a world in which animals literally resembled the common names we have bestowed upon them—and invited graphic designer Bill Noonan to help flesh out the fantasy.*

### October 1978

Linnaeus began the system of bestowing a two-part, Latin-based name on every living thing in the 18th century. Today, taxonomists debate proposed names for newly-discovered organisms, and established names are sometimes changed. Thus Galápagos tortoises have changed from *Testudo elephantopus* (elephant-footed tortoise) to *Geochelone elephantopus* (elephant-footed earth turtle)—a change which perhaps only a taxonomist could appreciate. Polar bears, formerly called

milksnake

*Thalarctos maritimus* or Arctic bear of the sea, are now *Ursus maritimus* because they are now deemed closer to other members of the bear family (*Ursidae*).

So all living things have been given, or will be given when concensus is reached, a binomial— a two-part name which is the same all over the world. The first part of the binomial is the name of the genus (*Homo*); the second is the species (*sapiens*). Some species may be further broken down into subspecies. Each genus belongs to a family (*Hominidae*) and each family is part of an order (Primates). Orders comprise a class (Mammalia) and classes comprise a phylum (Chordata). Phyla constitute a kingdom (Animalia). Thus, when one knows the scientific name, from the species and genus on up the taxonomic ladder, one may trace that species' family tree—in other words, its relationship to all other living things.

Yet the use of common names persists, even among scientists. Common names can be useful, because often they incorporate some indication of the animal's native range, behavior or other characteristics. Common names are often colorful and evocative. Who would not like to know better the noble macaw or the perfect lorikeet, to travel to the home of the snow leopard? Who could fail to be intimidated by the Komodo dragon?

But common names should never be taken too literally. What can happen when they are is illustrated here.

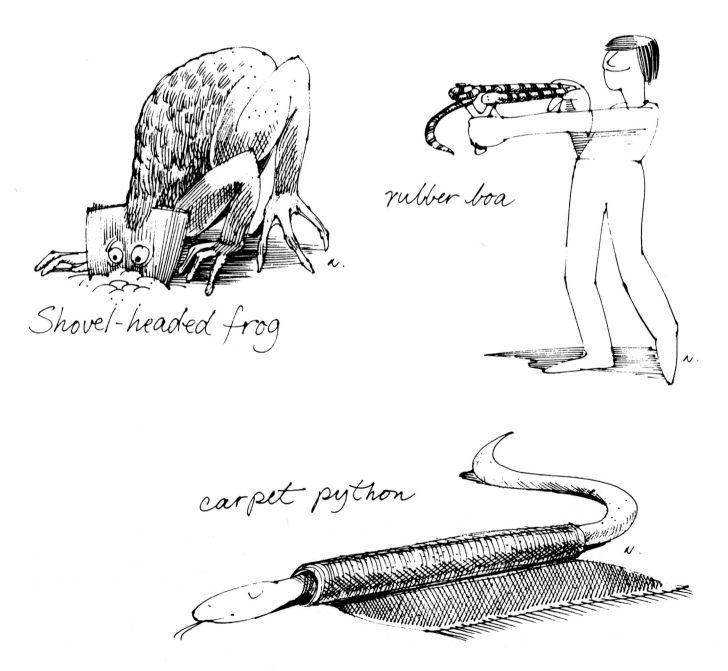

Shovel-headed frog

rubber boa

carpet python

_barking gecko_

_Sungazer_

# Believe It or Not—a Kiwi

## By Maureen L. Greeley

*The kiwi is a bird which doesn't fly, is nearly blind and spends most of its life in hiding. Small wonder it is one of nature's best-kept secrets. ZOONOOZ editorial assistant Maureen Greeley sheds some light on the reclusive fowl.*

**June 1983**

Perhaps it is not so difficult to understand why, historically, there has been some skepticism over the existence of a curious, nearly sightless bird that shuns daylight, has long whiskers emerging from the base of a beak one-third the length of its body (with nostrils at the tip of that bill), has a pair of useless rudimentary wings that are barely discernible beneath a coat of thick, hairlike feathers, and has no tail. Here is a bird that although flightless, can outdistance many dogs with its strong legs and sturdy feet, can burrow with the best of the groundhogs, and can put a chicken to shame with an egg equalling one-fifth to one-quarter of its own weight.

The kiwi (*Apteryx australis*) does in reality exist, unlike the mythical unicorn or the griffon. Friday, April 22, 1983, marked the first hatching of one of these interesting birds at the San Diego Zoo and only the second such hatching in the western hemisphere. This special hatching was the first fruit of a long, often frustrating effort to breed kiwis in San Diego.

On December 8, 1954, the Zoo received one kiwi, then the only one in the western hemisphere, from Auckland, New Zealand. This adult bird was named Belle, in honor of Belle Benchley, the Zoo's managing director emeritus.

It didn't seem to take Belle long to adjust to her California home. Belle took so well to the new environment, in fact, that she gave her keeper, Ernie Waggoner, and Kenton C. Lint, then curator of birds, quite a start when, not long after her arrival, she buried herself, as kiwis are wont to do, 18 inches deep within a peat-moss tunnel she had dug. Fearing that Belle had escaped or been stolen, K.C. and Ernie searched for 90 minutes, probing every inch of the enclosure before they discovered the curious creature.

Even more surprising was the later discovery that Belle was actually Benjamin! The difficulty in distinguishing sexes among kiwis was to present several problems, particularly in terms of establishing a breeding program over the years.

In 1969, the Zoo received a pair of kiwis—a 200th anniversary gift to the city of San Diego from the government of New Zealand—with hopes of starting a breeding program. The two kiwis were named Toa and Uha, or male and female in the language of New Zealand's native Maoris. Like Belle, Uha had difficulty living up to "her" name and, of course, the discovery that both kiwis were male did little to enhance the breeding program which, like the kiwis, never got off the ground.

It was not until 1979 that a genuine breeding program was started here, with kiwis from the San Diego Zoo, the National Zoo in Washington, D.C. (which had hatched a kiwi in 1975), and the Auckland Zoo. In 1983, the San Diego Zoo's first kiwi was hatched.

Females leave all rearing duties to the males once the eggs are laid (normally only one, sometimes as many as two or three). The father had been sitting on the egg at the Zoo for 71 days when the chick hatched. The hatchling was taken from the nest to prevent its being harmed in the nest box by the father's large feet.

Initially the chick is left in the incubator without food, as it feeds on yolk which has been stored in its abdomen. Because of the

*Maoris called the kiwi "the hidden bird" due to its love of privacy.*

*A rare glimpse of a rare bird, New Zealand's kiwi.*

high proportion of yolk in kiwi eggs (61 percent of the contents) they are believed to be the most nutritive of bird eggs. By the time feeding begins on day nine, the chick is expected to have lost 25 percent of its weight. On a diet of earthworms, chopped beef heart, assorted fruits and cereals, and a powdered vitamin and mineral supplement, the chick should regain its birth weight after only 10 to 15 days.

Young kiwis have essentially the same diet as the adults but consume smaller portions. When searching for earthworms, kiwis use their bills to probe the earth. Often this is accompanied by a loud sniffling sound as the birds exhale to clear dirt from the nasal passage. The kiwi's keen senses of smell and hearing are some compensation for poor eyesight. At night its range of sight is only six feet, and when daylight comes the kiwi can see no more than two feet beyond that long bill.

If frightened, the kiwi's best means of escape is its strong legs which carry the bird swiftly, if somewhat awkwardly. A pugnacious creature, the kiwi may choose to stay put and use those powerful legs and feet and his sharp claws for defense.

Female kiwis, at about five pounds, are somewhat larger than males. There is some variation in size between the three species. The scientific name *Apteryx* is derived from the Greek *a* meaning without and *pterux* meaning a wing. The common name kiwi was given to the birds by the native Maoris in imitation of the kiwi's calls. Kiwis rarely introduce themselves by name to anyone but another kiwi unless, of course, one happens to be in the damp New Zealand forests, or bush, after the sun has nearly set for the day. This characteristic led the Maoris to bestow upon the bird at least one more title—"the hidden bird."

Though the Maoris believed the kiwi to be protected by Tane, god of the forests, they killed the birds for sport and for food. The Maoris also prized the birds' soft, hairlike feathers for their most valuable ceremonial cloaks. These cloaks, known as *Kahu-Kiwi*, were made by weaving the feathers into a base of flax fibers. Occasionally, pure white examples of the North Island kiwi were found. The feathers from these birds were highly prized for adding borders and stripes to the ceremonial costumes.

White settlers prized the feathers, too—not for dress, but for trout flies. Kiwi leg bones were popular as well, for making pipestems. Kiwis were hunted most often at night using the kuri, or native dog, and torches, which served to stun and confuse the noctural birds. Man's encroaching civilization has done much to reduce the natural habitat of these bush-dwelling birds, believed extant for more than 8 million years. The kiwis' forest homes and their lives are further threatened by bush fires, which claim many of the birds each year.

New Zealand passed a law in 1908 prohibiting the hunting, capture, or killing of kiwis and in 1921 the kiwi was declared an "absolutely protected bird." The kiwi's popularity grew so that it was adopted as New Zealand's national emblem. Coins, postage stamps, fighting troops, and shoe polish all carry the name or image of the unique creature. New Zealanders themselves accepted the nickname "kiwis" given them by their allies during the Second World war. A bird that predates modern man by all but a few of its eight million years has finally impressed its significance on civilization.

# The Collared Lizard and His Blushing Bride

## By Susan Schafer

*It's true that the leopard can't change his spots—but the collared lizard can. It's all part of the mating game, according to Zoo keeper Susan Schafer, who files this report on romance among the reptiles.*

**July 1984**

Secret, and self-contained, and solitary as an oyster, the hero of our story is not unlike Dickens' Scrooge. He is the North American collared lizard (*Crotaphytus collaris*) scraping an hermitic existence from the hills and gullies of sun-drenched deserts.

Restricting his activity to a small home range on a rock outcropping or talus slope, he does not welcome intruders (unless they happen to be the proper size for a hearty meal). He readily exhibits his pomp to interlopers by arching his turquoise-colored back, puffing his black throat, and pumping his yellow chest up and down with his front legs in the traditional saurian push-up display.

Normally, he displays from the top of a prominent rock but, like the proverbial actor accepting a call for a command performance,

he acts whenever he is confronted in his own territory. At close quarters, he may gape threateningly, revealing a jet black mouth and a seemingly bottomless pit.

His culinary tastes bear out his pugnacious demeanor, for he is a voracious predator. His head is extremely broad in relation to his body and tail, as if Mother Nature ran out of the proper size and stuck on an oversized one in a pinch. He will eat almost anything that he can fit into his cavernous mouth including lizards, small snakes, spiders, and insects.

Swift, agile, and an excellent leaper, climber, and sprinter, he sounds like a candidate for the summer Olympics. He can run bipedally in open terrain by lifting his front legs off the ground and propelling himself by his back legs.

Even our super-saurian, faster than a speeding coyote and able to leap tall boulders in a single bound, has his problems to contend with and he must avoid falling to a snake or bird predator, such as the equally fleet-footed roadrunner.

Having survived the trials of summer, defended his territory and gorged upon his meals like a jaguar on a Brazilian plain, the collared lizard (named for the black bands encircling his neck) burrows deep beneath the rocks to spend the winter in characteristic solitude.

Around April, he emerges from his confinement to bask in lone luxury upon his favorite rock in the long-missed rays of the sun. But even this crusty old bachelor changes his ways once each year, and as spring blossoms it's not long before his mind turns to courting an attractive she-lizard.

Unlike the grandiloquent male, the female is dull gray or brown for most of the year. The male, however, sees only beauty and wastes no time in strutting about, bobbing his head and dashing toward his *objet d'amour*.

If the female is not receptive to the male's seductive advances, she flattens her body, snobbishly raises her tail, and walks away stiff-leggedly as if thoroughly disgusted with the

*A female collared lizard demonstrates her post-nuptial coloration.*

Susan Schafer

Susan Schafer

*A male collared lizard in his desert domain.*

whole affair. If, on the other hand, she is attracted to the eager male, she will allow him to bite her on the back of the neck as he mounts her and turn his tail under hers to achieve union.

But the honeymoon is over almost as soon as it began as the fickle male leaves to return to a bachelor's life. The female, however, is not discouraged. Instead, within a day or two after copulation, she shows off her newly acquired trousseau as the sides of her body become embellished with brilliant orange spots.

The post-nuptial coloration, like the gold band on a woman's left ring finger, warns other males away and keeps them from wasting their time and energy on a female who has already been taken care of. At the same time, it guarantees the female's faithfulness to our all-but-faithful hero and ensures that only his progeny will be born.

Our blushing June bride wears her adornment for several weeks as the now-fertilized eggs continue their development inside her body. In late June or July, she lays four to nine plump grapelike eggs and, soon after, her orange spots fade, abandoning her to her original drab wardrobe.

By August, the hatchlings make their appearance, but the kids are "kicked out of the house" to fend for themselves and must disperse into unoccupied areas before becoming a main course for mom or pop.

A variety of other reptiles don wedding colors in the spring. Female leopard lizards also blush spotted orange after mating and, like the collared lizards, advertise their unavailability.

In most cases, it is only the male who puts on nuptial dress and shows off, trying to titillate the senses of any female that will pay attention to him.

Interestingly enough, researchers have found that with the lizard species they studied painting additional color onto the male elevates his position in his respective hierarchy, increasing his conspicuousness and probably his success at attracting a female as well. The smart dresser, it seems, has the edge in the mating game.

But with the passing of spring, so passes the glitter of the season, and we find among the many wild creatures our hero, the collared lizard, facing the prospects of another winter alone.

# The Mysterious Tiger From Tasmania

## By Steven Joines

*The thylacine, Tasmania's marsupial wolf, is generally believed to be extinct. However, recent evidence suggests that a few may yet survive. Animal researcher Steven Joines traces the tortured history of this intriguing and possibly vanished animal.*

**September 1983**

For reasons not clearly understood, placental mammals had not colonized Australia by the time that the island continent became isolated from the earth's other land masses. Free from competition with the more advanced placental mammals, Australia's marsupial mammals were able to fill every available ecological niche.

One of the most striking examples is the thylacine, also known as the marsupial wolf. The thylacine stands two feet at the shoulder, grows to more than six feet in overall length, and is amazingly wolflike in appearance. The thylacine is the largest carnivorous marsupial known to have existed within historic times.

In prehistoric times the range of the thylacine included New Guinea, mainland Australia, and Tasmania. However, the early introduction of the dingo by aboriginal colonizers caused the extinction of thylacines on New Guinea and the mainland. The thylacine's relatively stiff, kangaroolike tail causes the species difficulty in maneuvering quickly, a distinct disadvantage for competition with true dogs.

The thylacine population of Australia was eradicated within a thousand years of the dingo's introduction. Only on the island of Tasmania, where dingos were never introduced, has the marsupial wolf survived into modern times.

However, one of the great modern zoological mysteries is whether or not the thylacine does, in fact, survive. Since the death of the last captive specimen, on September 7, 1936, very little in the way of hard evidence has been produced to confirm the continued existence of the species. Today the thylacine is officially listed as extinct though the species certainly survived into the 1960s, and there remains hope that small numbers of thylacines may yet be found inhabiting the densely forested tracts of Tasmania's unpopulated west coast.

The first European to record the existence of the thylacine was the Dutch mariner Abel Janszoon Tasman. On December 2, 1642,

*The thylacine demonstrates its ability to open its jaws wider than any other mammal.*

National Zoological Park, Smithsonian Institute

Tasman noted in his journal that a shore party had observed, "Certain footprints of animals, not unlike those of a tiger's claws." (On Tasmania the thylacine is widely known as "the tiger," in reference to the 14 to 18 dark brown or black stripes that adorn its fawn to grayish-brown coat.)

In 1807, G.P. Harris gave the tiger the binomial name *Didelphis cynocephala* (wolf-headed opossum) but the following year saw the name amended to *Thylacinus cynocephalus* (pouched dog with wolf head).

Unfortunately, Harris's brief description was virtually the only scientific interest in the species until well into the twentieth century. By 1838, the number of sheep in Tasmania had exceeded one million, and the wool and mutton industries had become Tasmania's main sources of revenue. With the expansion of sheep-ranching activities, tigers and ranchers came into ever-increasing conflict.

A systematic extermination campaign that was to last for 69 years was launched. By the 1840s it was common practice to shoot tigers on sight.

No one is certain how plentiful thylacines were when Europeans first settled permanently on Tasmania. Although the island's carrying capacity probably never allowed a substantial population, thylacines were apparently well dispersed. The tiger's preferred habitat is broken country, savanna woodland, river flats, and button-grass plains where rocky outcrops are available to provide shelter during daylight hours.

Tasmanian tigers are almost exclusively nocturnal in their habits, Normally, they are solitary hunters, though pairs have been seen hunting together. To track down prey, tigers rely primarily on a keen sense of smell.

Upon picking up the scent of a kangaroo or wallaby, the tiger will trot after its prey relentlessly. Such chases may last many hours before the intended victim is brought to bay, exhausted. At this point, the tiger makes a final, quick charge and characteristically dispatches its prey by the unique method of biting off a piece of its skull. This unusual killing strategy is facilitated by the thylacine's ability to gape its jaws as wide as 120 degrees, wider than any other known mammal.

Like all marsupials, female thylacines give birth to naked, poorly developed young. The young, numbering one to four, are initially nutured in the female's pouch. Because the normally solitary female needs to be mobile

*A pair of thylacines at the National Zoological Gardens in Washingtion, around the turn of the century.*

and untiring to function successfully as a predator, the young are probably retained in the pouch only as long as is absolutely necessary to assure their survival. After approximately three months, females cache their offspring in a rock shelter or some other secluded spot and return to feed them at intervals.

By the mid-1880s, the anti-tiger sentiments of Tasmania's sheep ranchers were running so high that a petition to eradicate the thylacine was introduced to Parliament. In 1888 the government introduced a bounty scheme. Tiger hunting became a lucrative side line for many Tasmanians. Between 1888 and 1909, 2,184 thylacine skins were officially presented for payment. This figure, however, is certainly far below the actual number of animals killed, because some property owners offered private bounties of their own.

The mid-19th century saw the introduction of fur trapping in the more inaccessible regions of Tasmania, where the bulk of the thylacine population had been driven by sheep ranchers. While the tiger was of casual interest as a bounty animal, trapping reduced the thylacine's food supply.

The cumulative effects of hunting and trapping contributed to driving tigers away from their preferred savanna habitat and into the dense forests of the west coast. The final blow, however, was not linked to direct human predation. Beginning around 1905, an outbreak of disease, possibly distemper introduced by domestic dogs, swept through Tasmania. The disease caused a drastic decline in the thylacine population, and by 1914, the species was poised on the brink of extinction. The last thylacine killed in the wild whose death was reported, was shot on May 13, 1930.

Since 1938, several expeditions have been undertaken in an effort to confirm the tiger's survival. Concentrated primarily on the northern part of the island, several of these have produced plaster casts of footprints and other circumstantial evidence but, to date, the tigers themselves have remained elusive. Nevertheless, more than 300 sightings of thylacine-like animals have been reported since 1936, and reports of sightings continue to filter out of the Tasmanian bush.

Beginning in 1979, the Australian National Parks and Wildlife Services, undertook an ambitious search for the thylacine. The project failed to secure any evidence of the tiger's survival.

In 1966, the government that once actively sought to exterminate the species set aside 1,600,000 acres in the South-West District as a sanctuary for the thylacine.

*The thylacine's stripes caused the marsupial to be called the "Tasmanian tiger."*

Karel Havlicek/Zoobooks

*(preceding page) African bush elephant (Loxodonta african africana)*

*(upper left) Chester, an Alaskan brown bear (Ursus arctos gyas) who died in 1985, was probably the most photographed animal in Zoo history. Shown here in a typical pose, he was the star attraction on the bus tour for many years where he endeared himself to the public and Zoo personnel alike by never failing to perform for every passing audience.*

*(upper right) Altai Wapiti (Cervus elaphus sibiricus). Photo by Lou Ann Hecker*

*(below) African lion (Panthera leo). Photo by Kenneth Fink*

*(opposite page) Meerkats (Suricata suricatta). Photo by R. Van Nostrand*

(upper left) Indo-Chinese leopard
(Panthera pardus delacouri).
Photo by Kenneth Fink

(upper right) Bolivian red howler
monkey (Alauatta seniculus sara).
Photo by R. Van Nostrand.

(below) Indian rhinoceros
(Rhinoceros unicornis)

# Landscaping for Animals

## By Charles Coburn

*Animals, like people, respond to their environment positively or negatively. Keeping the zoo animal happy and healthy requires careful planning when it comes to creating its enclosure as horticulturalist Charles Coburn points out.*

**January 1984**

When we introduce animals into our zoological garden, we assume the responsibility for their well being. Our degree of knowledge and sensitivity, and our values all direct the techniques of animal husbandry we employ and the quality of the new environment which we are able to provide the animals.

Public attitudes toward animals are affected a great deal by the environments in which those animals are exhibited. In a more natural environment, the animal's grace, dignity, and inherent value are perceived as being greater. Conversely, the obviously caged animal, confined in an unnatural enclosure, is perceived as possessing less desirable characteristics—gracefulness decreases, freedom decreases, and happiness, dignity, and naturalness decrease.

When landscaping for humans, the first thing to be learned is what the client wants. The same is true for the animal client. We seek to understand the needs of the animal and its potential range of behaviors. Necessary elements for expression of that behavior can then be incorporated into the enclosure. These might include watercourses, wading pools, logs for scratching or clawing, perches, sunning rocks, or a space for a courtship ritual. A review of the animal's natural habitat guides decisions on required enclosure space, the orientation of that space to the sun and prevailing winds, and whether a flat, sloping, or rolling area is preferable. Further, it guides selection of plant materials. Ideally, the same plant species which occur in the wild are used to landscape the enclosure. If wild species are

unavailable, plants with similar characteristics are substituted. Plants are also selected with regard to their insect resistance.

A means of irrigating the plants is incorporated into the landscape design. Generally, two independent systems are installed; each one provides water for half the enclosure. One system is operated at a time so that the animals may always move out of the water flow. These systems are also used to settle dust and to cool animals in warm weather. If the soil drains, irrigation water can aid dilution and dispersion of animal-deposited salts.

It is estimated that approximately 2,000 years are required to produce a single inch of topsoil. This rich soil is a scarce commodity in many animal exhibits. Soil compaction, the result of animal traffic, is common. When this occurs, rain or irrigation water puddles or runs off, taking with it the thin layer of topsoil. Compacted soil contains less air space and fewer beneficial microorganisms. There is also a greater potential for root disease in compacted soil.

To some extent, this process of compaction can be countered by periodic introduction of organic matter to the soil accompanied, in some cases, by rototilling.

There is much to be considered as we move from the static environments of stark concrete or decomposed granite to the constantly changing environments of landscaped exhibits. These more complex, integrated plant and animal systems require closer monitoring and greater care if they are to be successful. We believe that the benefits to the animals make them worthwhile.

*A siamang in his island home at the Zoo.*

# Why Plants?

## By Michael Bostwick

*The tendency is to take plants for granted and assign them a secondary role in the scheme of things. Landscape supervisor Michael Bostwick reminds us of plants' often-overlooked contributions to our lives—and, in fact, to our very existence.*

**June 1985**

What do plants mean to humankind? They provide, in many cases, a green backdrop for our lives, but their importance goes far beyond that. Man has learned to domesticate and cultivate plants, using them and their by-products for food, clothing, medicine, cosmetics, wood products, spices, latex, and waxes. He has even learned how to dig and drill into the earth's surface to retrieve fossil fuels supplied by decaying plant materials. These fuels are sources of energy that we have come to depend on to support our various means of transportation and to provide us with warmth.

Fossil records show that plants such as palms, hickories, oaks, beans, breadfruit, magnolias, grapes, and tulip trees flourished 60 to 70 million years ago. These plants helped provide ancient peoples with their food and shelter. Evidence indicates that corn was first cultivated nearly 5,000 years ago in Mexico. Approximately 1,500 years later, potatoes were cultivated in South America, and rice was introduced to the Far East.

At one time, 60 percent of the world's coastlines in tropical areas were covered with mangroves. Today that percentage has dropped to less than one percent. Mangroves act as an important link in our food chain, providing breeding grounds for fishes. Mangroves and their by-products provide food, medicines, firewood, lumber, dyes, resin for plywood adhesive, and viscose, which is used in the production of rayon fabric. Unfortunately, the desire for these products may eventually lead to the destruction of the remaining mangroves.

Jojoba is another plant that is now well known in our society because its oil is used in cosmetic products and as a lubricant for engines. It has a very high melting point, as does another similar product—whale oil. Killing whales for their oil certainly seems senseless when we can harvest the jojoba nut.

Plants have always been used to help heal man's ills; today they are used extensively in the creation of medicines to combat disease.

Parks and gardens provide a system of fresh air channels that funnel clean, cool air into and through our cities. In fact, the most important role of plants on earth is as oxygen producers. An actively growing grass plot of 25 square feet will release enough oxygen to sustain the daily life of an adult. Plants also absorb many pollutants, control soil erosion, dissipate heat, and provide beauty and areas for recreation.

Many plants in their habitats are endangered, especially in the tropical rain forests. There have been nearly 500,000 tropical plants identified; these represent less than one-sixth of what we believe the tropical areas hold. There are probably countless plants waiting to be discovered—some might possibly hold the cure for our most serious diseases or become new food sources.

A 1980 estimate indicates that areas equaling the size of Great Britain are vanishing from the tropical forests each year through destruction. If that rate continues, they could be eliminated completely in approximately 36 to 50 years. In Madagascar, for example, only seven percent of the natural vegetation remains. There are as many as 7,000 plants in this area that grow nowhere else on earth.

Growing populations make difficult demands on these tropical areas. Farm land is important to these populations, and a single person can clear a hectare of forest in twelve days using an ax.

So, plants play many roles in our lives. They have the potential to heal, to warm, to shelter, to calm, and to sustain life. They are intriguing and useful, beautiful and versatile.

Why plants? They are an undeniably important part of our life.

*The jojoba, whose seed contains oil similar to that of the sperm whale.*

# Overcutting Tropical Rain Forests: Undercutting our Daily Lives?

## By Norman Myers, Ph.D.

*Current estimates are that the earth's tropical rain forests are vanishing at the rate of 100 square miles per day, perhaps more. The possibly catastrophic effects of this destruction are explored by Dr. Norman Myers, one of the world's leading authorities on the environment.*

**October 1981**

The chain saws keep buzzing, the bulldozers keep rumbling, the fires keep burning. Through the hand of the commercial logger, the cattle rancher, and, most of all, the subsistence cultivator, tropical rain forests are falling with every tick of the clock.

Where are the trees toppling fastest? The number one area, being worked over by thousands of timber corporations (some of them giant concerns based in North America, Japan, and Western Europe) and by at least 150 million small-scale farmers, is Southeast Asia, notably the Philippines, Indonesia, and Malaysia. A similarly rapid trend is overtaking rain forests from southern Mexico through Central America to Panama, though here the main factor is the cattle rancher, producing "cheap" beef for the fast-food chains of North America. There is little undisturbed forest left in most countries of West Africa, especially those two leading forest countries, Sierra Leone and Liberia. Rather, there is extensive secondary forest—a wildlife-impoverished form of forest that replaces primary, or virgin, forest. By the end of the 1980s, West Africa could well have seen the last of its original forest formations, with their extreme abundance and diversity of plants, birds, butterflies, mammals, amphibians, and the rest.

To all of which, an average American, may reflect that, sad as the story sounds for wildlife enthusiasts, it is really too remote from everyday life to excite much concern.

Let us take a quick look at some surprising linkages between the work of the chain saw thousands of miles away from Los Angeles, London, and Tokyo, and the routine welfare of Los Angeles and the rest.

Tropical rain forests are reckoned to harbor two-fifths of earth's five to ten million species. If, as appears a likely prospect, one-half of all tropical rain forests become grossly disrupted if not destroyed outright by the end of the century, this could mean a loss of one million species in these forests—many more than in all other ecological zones put together!

It is by grace of wild plant germ plasm from tropical forests that we receive much of our daily bread. Rain forest species have supplied the origins of many staple foods, notably rice, corn, millet, bananas, and sugar cane. Wild relatives of these major crops supply genetic variations to boost productivity and disease resistance of croplands throughout North America, Western Europe, the Soviet Union, and Japan.

Among recent exciting discoveries is a wild form of corn, discovered in a montane forest of central Mexico. This plant's disease resistance and perennial growth traits may boost productivity for corn growers throughout the world and reduce prices for corn consumers. By consumers, we mean each of us whenever we enjoy an omelette for breakfast, a pork escalope for lunch, an outsize steak for dinner; also each time we read a magazine, mail a letter, drink a beer or a soft drink or a bourbon, eat candy, chew gum, light a match, wash our face, paint our house, take an aspirin, apply cosmetics, utilize dynamite and, in gasohol sectors of the country, each time we drive our car.

In similar style, we benefit from rain forest relatives of modern crops each time we drink a cup of coffee, eat chocolate fudge, or enjoy a banana split. If the rain forests of the tropics eventually fade from the scene, we can expect plunging productivity and soaring prices for many food items.

Rain forests not only supply germ plasm material to support our existing crops, but also offer a huge cornucopia of further foods, if we can only identify them before the axe completes its work. A hitherto uncultivated fruit of Southeast Asia, the mangosteen, has been described as "perhaps the world's best tasting

Phillip T. Robinson

*A rain forest giant falls to make way for a farmer's crops.*

Each time we take a prescription from our doctor to the neighborhood pharmacy, there is one chance in four that the medication we collect owes its origin to start-point materials of plants or animals from tropical rain forests.

Tropical rain forests constitute earth's main repository of drug-yielding plants. Around 2,000 species are thought to possess anti-cancer properties. In 1960, a child suffering from leukemia had only one chance in five of remission; now, thanks to drugs developed from the rosy periwinkle, native to Madagascar's rain forests, the child enjoys four chances in five. According to the Economic Botany Laboratory in Beltesville, Maryland, the forests of Amazonia alone could well contain plants with materials for five "anti-cancer superstar drugs."

Not only plants, but also insects, notably butterflies, offer potential for anti-cancer compounds,—and tropical rain forests harbor some 1.5 to 3.5 million insect species. Widespread elimination of tropical rain forests could represent a serious setback for the anti-cancer campaign.

As for other medicines, consider a small shrub native to tropical forests in India and Southeast Asia—the serpentine root. This plant has been used by local people for 4,000 years to treat snake bites, nervous disorders, and fevers. In the late 1940's the plant turned out to be a fine hypotensive agent, and by 1953 it was being used to relieve hypertension and schizophrenia. Shortly after that, its extract, reserpine, became the principal source of materials for tranquilizers. Before that time, high blood pressure strongly disposed a patient toward stroke, heart failure, or kidney failure; but today this one plant helps many millions of people to lead a reasonably normal and healthy life, practically freed from a set of ailments—hypertension— that constitutes the single greatest and fastest-growing source of mortality in advanced nations, notably in the United States.

Tropical rain forests yield a wide variety of specialist materials for industrial use. From Southeast Asia's forests alone we derive latex, gums, camphor, damnor, resins, dyes, and ethereal oils. Many rain forest plants bear oil-rich seeds, for example, the babassu palm, the seji palm, and a number of other trees that grow wild in Amazonia. The babassu's fruit contains up to 72 percent oil, which can be used to produce fibers, cattle feed, soap, detergents, starch, and general edibles.

The babassu's fruit can also serve as a substitute for diesel oil. Similarly, the "petroleum nut" of the Philippines produces a highly volatile oil, and was used by the Japanese as fuel during World War II. More recently, Nobel Prize-winning biochemist Professor Melvin Calvin, of Berkeley, has come

fruit." From rain forests of the same region comes a vine known as the Chinese gooseberry, which bears fruit with juice 15 to 18 times richer in vitamin C than orange juice.

Tropical rain forests can also help to keep down the numerous pests that reduce the amount of food grown around the world. Despite an annual pesticide bill of several billion dollars, at least 40 percent of our crops are lost each year to insects and similar pests, both in the fields and in storage. A sound way to control insect pests is to utilize other insects that serve as predators and parasites. According to the U.S. Department of Agriculture, biological control programs that entail importation of counter-pest species from abroad into the United States return $30 for every $1 invested. Citrus growers in Florida, for example, have been able to save around $30 million a year through a one-time outlay of $35,000 for the importation of three types of parasitic wasps.

across a tree in the depths of Amazonia, with a sap so akin to fossil petroleum that it can go straight into the tank of a diesel engine, whereupon the truck fires immediately and drives sweetly away.

Although we do not yet have conclusive scientific evidence, there are signs that widespread burning of tropical rain forests could affect climatic patterns in temperate zones.

When a patch of forest is burned, much of the immense stocks of carbon in the plants and in the soil are released into the atmosphere in the form of carbon dioxide. At the current rate of increase of carbon dioxide buildup, the "natural" amount, that is, the amount in the atmosphere until about the middle of the last century, could well double by the year 2030 or soon thereafter.

True, conventional wisdom believes that the main source of carbon dioxide lies with those massive consumers of fossil petroleum—factories and automobiles. More recently, however, evidence has been accumulating that tropical forests could be a sizable source.

The consequences of carbon dioxide buildup could be severe. Because of the greenhouse effect of carbon dioxide in the atmosphere, the earth's temperature is rising. Twice as much carbon dioxide in the atmosphere could well cause an average global increase of two to three degrees Celsius, a greater temperature change than has occurred during the past 10,000 years. By consequence, there would probably be warmer and drier weather in North America, especially in the great grain-growing belt. A temperature increase of only one degree Celsius could decrease United States corn production by 11 percent—with all that implies for America's capacity to feed itself and millions of persons starving in the Third World.

Such, then, is the linkage between the fate of tropical forests and our daily lives. Let us not forget that we are all, in our various ways, contributing to the problem: through our demand for tropical hardwoods and "cheap" (noninflationary) beef and through our support, as marketplace investors, for giant timber corporations that extract their timber harvests in an unduly disruptive manner.

If the forests disappear we shall all suffer, not only those of us in the tropical countries concerned, but also those of us who enjoy a varied diet, who partake of modern medicines, and who enjoy a growing array of manufactured goods from innovative industry.

In this double regard, we should all contribute to a campaign in support of tropical forests—not out of a sense of further charity for Third World contries, but out of a sense of joint responsibility for a deteriorating asset of global heritage.

# The Frozen Botanical Garden

## By Bob Ward

*Cryogenic preservation of animal cells and tissue has already proved its value (See "Our Frozen Zoo," page 87). Now, as horticultural assistant Bob Ward reports, the same technique is being used to preserve certain plant species.*

**March 1983**

The frozen zoo of the future will include more than animals. Przewalski's horses and Arabian oryx probably will be sharing their cryogenically preserved arks with palms and ferns. Experimentation with cryogenic, or deep-freeze, methods of preserving plant cells is going on at a number of institutions, including the San Diego Zoo. The results suggest that these are promising methods of safeguarding from total extinction at least the most valuable members of the world's flora.

Cryogenic preservation is not an alternative to native habitat preservation. It is

*Cycad cones.*

viewed as a drastic measure that could provide an invaluable hedge against the immediate dangers of species destruction until more effective habitat conservation measures can be taken. Cryogenic preservation does have limitations. Some species cannot survive the dehydration process that must occur before successful freezing can take place. If water is not removed, large ice crystals, which may damage cell members, form during the freezing process.

Several vials of cycad pollen spores have already joined company with the Zoo's frozen animal cells. While these vials are only part of a fledgling study on preserving pollen for later use in the fertilization of the Zoo's cycads, similar techniques could be employed with other plant spores and seeds. Cryogenic preservation is being attempted with cycad pollen because mature cycads have difficulty producing fertile seeds through cultivation. For fertilization to occur both male and female cycads must be present. In addition, they must bear cones at specific times to enable successful transfer of pollen. This kind of timing rarely occurs in collections of cultivated plants where coning is sporadic. At the Zoo, cycad pollen is collected, labeled, and cryogenically preserved with intentions of reviving appropriate species in the future to artificially fertilize mature female cones.

This concept is not entirely original—cycad pollen had been successfully stored under refrigeration before, but not at temperatures as low as $-190°$ C ($-310°$ F). At this temperature, cellular changes virtually stop, enabling indefinite storage periods. The security of long term germ plasm stability allows the possibility of establishing a permanent collection bank of materials. Freezing revivable germ plasma from endangered plants may actually be simpler and less costly than attempting to keep species alive through persistent cultivation.

Freezing large seeds such as coconuts may present some problems. But tissue grown from plant cells cultured in sterile media has been cryogenically preserved. This technique, although more difficult, may provide yet another form of species conservation. The genes of economically important sterile hybrid food plants also require this kind of treatment.

Someday, perhaps, botanical gardens will conserve much larger plant collections than they actually cultivate. Valuable endangered plants that are difficult to cultivate or of poor ornamental quality will be kept "on ice," available as required. Cryogenic preservation and cultivation of species in botanical collections both play important roles in conservation efforts. These, however, should not be viewed as alternatives to the optimum method of protecting species in their natural habitats.

*Encephalartos ferox cone, showing pollen sacs.*

*(preceding page) Australian flame pea (Chorizema ilicifolium)*

*(this page) Borzicactus (Borzicactus sp.). Photo by R. Van Nostrand*

*(opposite page) Foxglove (Digitalis)*

*(following page) Blue hibiscus (Alyogyne huegelii)*

# The Giant's Outlook

## By Charles E. Shaw

*The dwindling numbers of the giant Galápagos tortoises caused a number of zoos to attempt to preserve the species by captive reproduction. The San Diego Zoo was one of the few to succeed. Charles E. Shaw, the curator of reptiles, paused in 1968 to take stock of the past and assess the future.*

**November 1968**

It was on October 21, 1958, that five young Galápagos tortoises made their unexpected, overwhelming appearance. The long wait had suddenly come to an end as the ebony-shelled youngsters crowded one another in a large sand-filled crock. The tortoise eggs had been deposited and tended there since being laid the previous February 16.

The advent of these youngsters raised our hopes—we were on the right track in our effort to induce the Galápagos tortoises to produce fertile eggs. For many years we had incubated clutch after clutch of eggs only to be thwarted and disappointed by their constant infertility. Then we had the notion that the adobe soil of the enclosure, because of extreme hardness, was perhaps placing some obstacle in the way of the normal course of events for these cumbersome creatures. In 1957, the soil in the eastern one-third of the tortoise enclosure was dug out and replaced to a depth of about 40 inches with river sand. Whether this did the trick, we cannot definitely say. At least Galápagos tortoise eggs began hatching, and the female tortoises certainly must have been happier with the much more convenient nursery pasture.

Since 1958, we have attempted the incubation of every whole Galápagos tortoise egg that came our way together with a few that were not completely intact. During the laying process the female feels obliged to pause occasionally to arrange the eggs in the nest with one or both of her clumsy back feet. These seemingly insensitive instruments cause a considerable amount of cracking as well as breaking. Also the unlucky eggs that happen to fall into the nest first are most likely to suffer some damage to their thick calcareous shells through merely having succeeding eggs dropped upon them. As this is a common occurrence, it almost appears as if it were Nature's way of keeping the Galápagos tortoise population

*A baby Galápagos tortoise emerges from its shell.*

within its proper bounds. For example, of a clutch of twenty eggs laid by a female on April 17, all appeared to be good. However, after the successful hatching of four young tortoises from this clutch of eggs the remainder were examined. At least fourteen were definitely cracked. Even more frustrating was the fact that nine of the fourteen cracked eggs proved to be fertile, containing dead embryos in varying stages of development.

When possible we have someone on hand during the actual laying of the eggs. This involves considerable time and patience, but it was thought that if the eggs have no chance to drop into or onto anything more unyielding than a human hand there would appear to be little chance for them to suffer any mishap. Such is not the case, however. Recently two eggs deposited directly into the human hand, one after the other, were both cracked. Presumably these eggs could have been cracked only as the result of pressure upon each other while still in the female's oviduct.

# A Tortoise Goes Home

## By James P. Bacon, Ph.D.

*The aim of captive breeding is not merely to preserve endangered species but to return them to their native environment whenever possible. One such successful mission is described by Dr. James Bacon, general curator of herpetology.*

**February 1978**

Islas Galápagos—even the name of this world-famous archipelago refers to its best known residents: the giant tortoises.

You don't know much about the Galápagos Islands? Then let me introduce you to one of the world's most fascinating places and an old friend whom I envy—since he has returned home to Galápagos after many years of visiting with us at the San Diego Zoo. This long-term visitor is a male Galápagos tortoise from Española Island (called Hood Island by some).

Española is but one of thirteen larger and many smaller islands which make up the Galápagos chain. The islands cluster about the equator 600 miles west of Ecuador. Volcanic activity was responsible for the Galápagos land masses where lava in shades of red, black, brown, and gray dominate the landscape. Although there is lush vegetation at the higher elevations, the predominating plants are the durable types of shrubs and cacti that we often associate with chaparral and desert communities.

Since the Galápagos Islands are so far from other land masses, the plants and animals that live there adapted to the special conditions present on the islands. Many of the plants and animals are found only in Galápagos. Some of these are sunflower relatives 30 or 40 feet tall; lizards that swim out to sea to feed on algae found on the ocean floor; a finch that uses cactus spines to feed like a woodpecker; and, of course, the giant tortoises.

No one knows when the tortoises arrived on the islands or from where they came. Probably all evolved from one colonizing population which arrived from South America hundreds of thousands of years ago. Even though the tortoises perhaps eventually colonized ten islands, and each island had at least one distinct tortoise population, the tortoises all look a great deal alike.

On Española, a low, flat, rock island with sparse vegetation, the tortoises have shells which are very high in front, long necks and

*Darwin Research Institute*

*Galápagos tortoise No. 21.*

long legs, a combination that enables them to reach high for food. They are somewhat smaller than their huge cousins on some of the other islands.

Until mankind set foot on the islands, the tortoises apparently lived a life of relative ease. Early records indicate large numbers of tortoises on most islands where they occurred.

The human species has brought about many changes, some accidentally and some on purpose. Men at sea during the 17th, 18th

and 19th centuries had difficulty keeping sufficient meat in their larders; they found that tortoises were easy to catch and could be kept alive for months in the holds of their ships, with no care whatever. Thousands were captured to feed the sailors.

Perhaps worse was the introduction to the islands of our domestic dogs, cats, goats, pigs, cattle and donkeys. Anywhere man goes, rats and mice also accompany him. These animals were soon living in the wild and causing trouble for the native Galápagos plant and animal species.

The tortoises were particularly defenseless. Dogs, cats, rats and pigs eat eggs and young tortoises up to 10 or 15 years of age. Donkeys, cattle and especially goats eat the same plant food the tortoises do, only more effectively and faster.

At least two, possibly three and perhaps four or more tortoise populations have been wiped out. On Española, the goats are the most severe problem. In the 1950s, the Charles Darwin Research Station was built on Galápagos by the World Wildlife Fund. Studies began on the tortoises and much work has been done towards saving most of the populations. The tortoise rearing facility was built largely with money from the Zoological Society of San Diego.

There were so few animals of some populations that the males and females could not find each other during the mating season. Such was the case on Española. In order to maximize breeding potential, all of the tortoises that could be found on Española were taken to the research station. Sadly, only twelve females and two males were found.

Fifty years ago some scientists were so concerned about the future of the Galápagos tortoises that they organized expeditions to collect tortoises for distribution to zoos where it was hoped they would breed, thereby ensuring the survival of the species. This effort has not been totally rewarding. Only the Honolulu Zoo and the San Diego Zoo have had noteworthy success breeding these tortoises.

Tortoises arrived in San Diego from Española Island in 1934 and 1936. When the plight of the Española tortoises became known, we had only one male left. The Zoo attempted to return him to his birthplace but met with opposition because it could not be proven that the tortoise came from Española.

In 1976, we were able to verify that this was indeed an Española tortoise. With identity established, it was time to begin planning for the return trip of number 21 male. The tortoise was due to depart on July 9, 1977. However, after depositing the tortoise safely at the airport, we were met by a telegram upon our return to the Zoo.

The airplane scheduled to transport the

*Darwin Research Institute*

tortoise from the Ecuadorian mainland to Galápagos was inadequate for the task. We hurried back to the airport and retrieved the traveler ten minutes before his scheduled departure.

Finally, number 21 left on Monday, August 1, 1977. He made the last leg of his journey from the mainland to Academy Bay on the cruise ship Iguana. On 8 August, a Galápagos National Park crew uncrated the well-traveled tortoise in his quarantine corral at the Darwin Research Station.

*The traveling tortoise is released into his enclosure.*

*Darwin Station's rearing pen on Hood Island.*

*Jerry Staedeli*

*No. 21 is carried to a corral, his new home on Santa Cruz Island.*

# Ssu-pu-hsiang...

## *with the tail of an ass, the hoofs of a cow, the neck of a camel and the antlers of a stag... the four unlikes.*

### By James M. Dolan, Jr., Ph.D.

*While man has unquestionably been responsible for the destruction of many species, there is a growing number which owe their existence to his enlightened concern. Prominent among them is Pére David's deer whose peril-laden past and new secure future are reviewed by Dr. James Dolan, general curator of mammals.*

**December 1970**

Our knowledge of Pére David's deer began on a bleak September day in 1865, when Pére Armand David climbed the wall surrounding the Imperial Hunting Park near Peking to discover large numbers of this deer living in a state of semi-domestication.

Armand David was the son of an eminent doctor in the French Pyrenees. As a small boy, he was keenly interested in natural history but his burning ambition was to become a priest. Therefore, in 1850, Armand David took his vows in the Congregation of the Mission, founded by St. Vincent de Paul.

His ambition was to be a missionary in China, which had prompted his joining the Vincentian Community. His wish was not fulfilled until 1862, when he set sail for China. Prior to his departure, he was commissioned by the Muséum National d'Histoire Naturelle, Paris, to make a collection of zoological and botanical specimens.

Pére David was stationed in China from 1862 until 1874. At the time of his death in 1900 at the age of 74, he had discovered 58 birds, approximately 100 new insects, and a large number of mammals, including the golden monkey, the giant panda, and the deer which bears his name. He is also responsible for the introduction of many new species of plants which are now familiar in our gardens.

The Imperial Hunting Park was situated outside the south wall of the city of Peking. It

*A Pére David's deer enjoys a meditative moment poolside at the Wild Animal Park.*

*Pére David's deer, also known as milu.*

was a park of vast area surrounded by a wall forty miles long. The Chinese Emperors used the park as a hunting preserve. Within the park were several villages where horses, cattle, and sheep were raised for the use of the court. Along with the Pére David's deer, other species of deer and the Mongolian gazelle were maintained for sporting purposes.

The park was strictly guarded and Europeans were prohibited entry. Pére David was able to look over the wall and stated that he had seen over a hundred deer which resembled "long-tailed reindeer with very large horns." He was unable to obtain a specimen, but by bribing some of the Tartar soldiers who guarded the park, he acquired two skins which were forwarded to Paris.

What Pére David saw when he looked over the wall of the Park was an animal that had ceased to exist in the wild for some three to four thousand years and had survived in the state of semi-domestication for the pleasure of the Manchu emperors.

*A young Pére David's deer, born at the Wild Animal Park.*

M. Henri de Bellonet, Chargé d'Affaires of the French Legation in Peking was able to procure a pair of Pére David's deer from the Imperial Park, and he kept them for nearly two years in a court near the French Embassy.

When he returned to Paris in 1867, he learned that the London Zoological Society was interested in the animals and he agreed to let the Society have the deer if it would cover the cost of transportation. Unfortunately, both animals died before they could be shipped.

Sir Rutherford Alcock, of the British Legation, was successful in acquiring a young pair which reached London on the second of August, 1869, the first Pére David's deer to be received alive in Europe.

After this, other specimens were imported and bred in Europe, with the result that before the turn of the century, the species was represented in many of the larger Continental collections.

Fortunately, there were living examples in Europe when the flood waters of the Hun Ho river breached the wall of the Imperial Hunting Park in 1894, permitting most of the deer to escape into the surrounding countryside where they were killed and eaten by the famine-stricken peasants.

All the remaining game animals were scattered during the Boxer Rebellion in 1900. The walls of the Imperial Hunting Park were broken down in various places by the allied troops. Some of the animals were killed by the soldiers or captured and killed by the native farmers. After the 1911 Revolution and the abdication of the Manchu rulers in 1912, only two Pére David's deer remained in China. Both were dead by 1921. Thus, the long association of the Chinese with Pére David's deer came to an end.

The events in China prompted the 11th Duke of Bedford to establish a herd of Pére David's deer on his extensive estate, Woburn, in Bedfordshire, England. With the death of older animals in continental collections, Woburn became the only reservoir for the species.

Disaster nearly overtook the Pére David's deer during the First World War when starvation and disease reduced the herd to a mere remnant.

The tragedy came very near to being repeated during the Second World War except for the efforts of the 12th Duke and Mrs. Osborne Samuel, who took charge of the park department during those critical years.

With characteristic foresight, the 12th Duke decided that in maintaining all of the existing deer at Woburn, he was keeping all of the species eggs in one basket. Consequently, in 1946, he sent specimens to Whipsnade, the country estate of the London Zoological Society, as well as to the New York Zoological Park.

In 1949, specimens were sent to the Sydney Zoological Garden, and since that time representatives have made their way to many other collections. The year 1956 saw the return of Pére David's deer to China with the shipment of two males and two females to the Peking zoo. Thus the circle had made a complete turn.

Presently, the world population exceeds 400 (including those at San Diego) and its continuation can be considered assured.

# The California Condor—Forever a Symbol

## By Marjorie Betts Shaw

*The California condor stands at the top of the list of the world's endangered creatures. Despite determined efforts by conservationists, headed by the San Diego Zoo, the condor's plight remains desperate. ZOONOOZ editor Marjorie Shaw reviews this magnificent bird's unhappy relationship with man.*

**May 1983**

Its destiny from the beginning, perhaps, was to be a symbol. To modern man it symbolizes prehistory. Its kind has soared above North America since the Pleistocene. Fossils from that epoch at Rancho La Brea show that a forebear of the California condor shared the same period, the same habitat, and the same fate as the saber-tooth tiger. Who fails to be stirred by the thought that we, in this modern age of crowded cities and shrinking country, can still share space with a magnificent bird that has been linked to humankind since the beginning of man's existence in North America? The past is with us as long as there is a survivor among us, and the California condor binds us to an earlier, primordial world.

When man first entered the condor's realm, his relationship with this giant of the skies was mystical. Primitive spears and arrows couldn't reach a bird that flew so high, or with such speed, so the two species lived in harmony. Many Indian tribes united themselves by ritual with the condor because to them the bird symbolized immortality.

The condor soared above the North American wilderness for thousands of years with relatively few problems until civilization discovered the bird.

The first written record of the California condor appeared in 1602. Father Ascension, a Carmelite friar accompanying the Vizcaino expedition to California, reported a flock of the giant vultures feeding on a dead whale in Monterey Bay. Still, there was little disturbance to the condor's world until the 19th century, when explorers, settlers, and naturalists arrived. A gun was no primitive weapon to be easily avoided.

Settlers of the West regarded the birds as disease carriers and vermin. The slaughter had begun. Gold miners discovered that condor quills made good containers for gold dust. Students of natural science required specimens, and the killing continued.

Naturalists and explorers, though, had an appreciation for the bird that dominated the Western sky. Lewis and Clark saw their first condor at the mouth of the Columbia River. They called it the "beautiful buzzard of the Columbia," and Lewis's description and meticulous drawing of a condor's head was the first detailed account of a live California condor.

There are those who fail to recognize the condor as a symbol and a survivor of a once great, but lost, wilderness. The flurry of excitement over the two condor eggs brought to the Zoological Society's Avian Propagation Center and the subsequent hatching of those eggs elicited remarks such as "What do you mean nearly extinct? You said there were about 20 of them!" and "Why do we want to save them—they're just vultures."

One can only hope that this North American condor with the new severely limited range

*The California condor.*

will not become a symbol of extinction. In 1970 it was thought that 50 condors remained. In 13 years that number has dropped by more than half. The spectacular flight which once inspired vast numbers of Indians to worship the condor as a demigod now can only be appreciated by a few. Those few may be the last to witness a life form that has been here since our earliest beginnings. Who would not wish to see a dodo, a great auk, a moa, or a saber-tooth tiger? For the California condor there is still a chance.

Then in 1952, through the efforts of Zoo leader Belle Benchley, permission was given to the Zoological Society to capture a pair of condors for the purpose of captive breeding. But floods and snow kept condor from captor, and the permit was rescinded. Strong opposition from environmental groups resulted in the passage of a resolution by the State Legislature that no more condor trapping permits would be issued.

In the words of Bill Toone, a keeper on the condor project who is totally absorbed with the California condor, "It is through disagreement or simple lack of cooperation that 30 years later, we are just getting the ball rolling."

The informal group on captive propagation and reintroduction of California condors, which comprises several agencies, has set forth recommendations for the disposition of condor eggs or birds of any age which call for an attempt to keep captive condors in close proximity to cohorts of a similar age. In following this procedure, Xolxol, the chick that the Zoological Society of San Diego received from the wild in August 1982 was sent to the Los Angeles Zoo to be introduced to a juvenile that was captured for sex determination and tagging. Bad weather and poor health prevented that bird's release, and it now has Xolxol for a companion.

Condors received or hatched will be identified with appropriate Indian names, or names from the region the birds inhabit. Xolxol is the Chumash Indian word that means both condor and spirit of condor, reinforcing the mystical regard in which early man held the magnificent bird.

On Wednesday, March 30, the first California condor ever hatched in captivity emerged from its shell after receiving some assistance from staff members at the Society's Avian Propagation Center. Keepers assumed the roles of adult vultures, playing tape recordings of vulture sounds and tapping on the egg as a natural parent would do. The egg was misted with a saline solution as Cynthia Kuehler gently lifted the shell from the hatchling. Sisquoc, named for the Sisquoc Condor Sanctuary

*Kenneth W. Fink*

*A condor soars.*

and its surrounding area, was alert and responding to its surrogate parent—a condor hand puppet—within a short time.

On the afternoon of April 5, the day the second California condor egg hatched (also with assistance), nature provided a fitting salute to mark the occasion—thunder cracked and crashed and rolled above San Diego County. To ancient North Americans such a display meant the condor was flapping his wings. Nature had heralded the arrival of a new thunderbird.

When it seemed impossible for early man to kill them with primitive weapons, the condors became symbols. When it seemed impossible to save them, they became symbols again. Is it now symbolically important to man that he attempt to save what he has, perhaps, destroyed? Early naturalists killed to learn—today's naturalists preserve to maintain a laboratory for learning.

Perhaps future offspring of Sisquoc, Xolxol, and their kind will continue to glide above a big-cone spruce forest, and will continue to astound observers as they climb to 15,000 feet to soar above a storm. And perhaps some future generation will be able to say, with awe, "I have seen a condor."

*California condor country: last remnant of a once-vast range.*

# The Last of the Wild Horses

## By James M. Dolan, Jr., Ph.D.

*Hard to pronounce and harder to spell, Przewalski's horse is believed to be extinct in the wild and survives in captivity only through a rare example of international cooperation between nations, zoos and individuals. Dr. James Dolan, general curator of mammals, reports.*

**September 1966**

During the latter part of the 19th century, as the last European wild horses were neighing their swan song on the plains of European Russia, a startling scientific discovery was made many thousands of miles to the east on the windswept steppes of Mongolia.

When Col. N. Przewalski, a Pole in the service of the Imperial Russian Army, was traveling through the eastern portion of the Dzungarian Gobi, he was presented with the skin and skull of a hitherto unknown wild horse. Realizing the value of his material, Przewalski sent it to the Zoological Museum of the Academy of Sciences at St. Petersburg, where in 1881, the zoologist Poliakov named his horse *Equus przewalskii*.

Speculation arose in Europe as to the true origin and relationship of this horse. There were those scientists who considered it to be a hybrid between the Mongolian domestic pony and the Mongolian wild ass, therefore a mule; but they were bitterly opposed by the faction which believed it to be a truly wild horse.

With what little material there was stored in a Russian museum, it is understandable that questions pertaining to its parentage could easily arise. It was not until more museum material and living animals were brought to Europe that the questions were eventually

resolved. Przewalski's horse was not only a wild animal but quite probably one of the ancestors of our many domestic breeds.

The first living Przewalski's horses brought to Europe arrived in Russia in 1899. Three mares were taken to the estate of the Russian-German F. von Falz-Fein at Askania Nova in the Ukraine. Falz-Fein, like the Dukes of Bedford in England, maintained one of the largest private collections of living animals in the world.

Between 1899 and 1903, eleven foals were imported into Askania Nova. Unfortunately, only two mares survived. In 1905, the Czar presented Falz-Fein with a purebred stallion and the breeding of these horses commenced.

At the onset of the Russian Revolution, Falz-Fein was forced to flee to Germany, his estate becoming the property of the new Russian government. Breeding continued so that, between 1905 and 1942, 37 purebred foals were produced. Eleven of these were sent to other zoological gardens and institutions within Russia and abroad. The German occupation of the Ukraine during World War II brought an end to 37 years of successful breeding of both pure and crossbred animals. At the conclusion of hostilities, only a single mare of 1/8 Przewalski blood remained at Askania Nova.

All of the Przewalski's horses living in

captivity, with the exception of a mare at Ulan Bator, Mongolia, and a mare sent to Askania Nova from Mongolia in 1957, are derived from five importations made between 1899 and 1904. Three of these importations were made into Russia. The remaining two were undertaken by the famous German family of animal dealers, Hagenbeck, in 1901 and 1904. The importation of 1901 was by far the largest and most important. Twenty-eight foals (15 stallions and 13 mares) arrived safely in Hamburg.

The largest percentage of this first great Hagenbeck importation was sold to the Duke of Bedford, pairs also going to London, Manchester, Berlin, Halle, New York, and a stallion to Paris. New York, having sent their first animals to Cincinnati, imported another pair in 1904.

Although breeding went quite well for many years, the herds dwindled to single aged individuals or eventually died out. By the middle 1950's, Przewalski's horse was no longer represented in the zoological gardens of

*Herd of Przewalski's horses at the Wild Animal Park.*

The colt Vasiliy shares a quiet moment with his mother, Vata, and another mare.

Orlitza, the last-caught Mongolian wild horse.

the western hemisphere. Shortly thereafter the Chicago Zoological Garden at Brookfield imported a pair from Munich, followed by importation from the same source by Roland Lindemann of the Catskill Game Farm. The Chicago horses have never bred, but the Catskill herd has been prolific. Horses have been sent to Washington, Alberta, Los Angeles, Louisville and San Diego from the Catskill herd.

Today, Przewalski's horse is one of the world's rarest mammals. Prior to 1950, it was observed near the mountain ridges of the Baytag-Bogdo and Takhin-Shara-Nuru. However, an expedition sent to the area by the Peking Zoological Garden was unable to locate a single animal, although in 1959, the Mongolians did observe two small herds not exceeding twenty. Since that time, a Russian expedition could not find any of the animals located by the Mongolians, so it is quite possible that Przewalski's horse now is extinct in the wild state.

Extreme rarity and an interesting zoological position as the only living true wild horse have inspired the zeal expended in its preservation. Although its numbers still remain dangerously low, even with all mares kept breeding, there is no doubt that the zoological gardens of the world will once again play a leading role in the conservation of yet another vanishing species.

# Horse Trading and Behavioral Research Pay Off

## By Martha Baker

*One of the major problems in a captive reproduction program is to prevent inbreeding due to the small gene pool. How the challenge is being met in the case of Przewalski's horse is revealed by Martha Baker, public relations manager for the Wild Animal Park.*

**May 1984**

*The stallion Basil, Vasiliy's father.*

Vasiliy, a male Przewalski's horse was born early on the morning of February 28, 1984, after a normal gestation of 327 days, according to Rich Massena, a field services manager at the Wild Animal Park.

Massena has an avid interest in the health and welfare of Vasiliy. Exactly 11 months before this birth Vasiliy's father, 20-year-old Basil, attacked and bit Massena as he was trying to rescue another newborn colt, Vargo, from repeated aggressions by the stallion. Massena was hospitalized for several days with a crushed forearm and was off work for two months because of the accident. Despite Massena's heroic efforts to save the colt, Vargo died the following day from internal injuries.

Vargo and Vasiliy share the same mother, Vata, who arrived in the United States in July 1982 from the Ukrainian preserve at Askania Nova. Vargo was sired by a stallion in Moscow prior to Vata's departure for the United States.

After Vargo's death, Wild Animal Park officials began to analyze a previous Przewalski's colt death (December 1982) that had, for lack of any contrary evidence, been listed as stillborn. Suspicions grew that Basil also may have caused that death. Like Vargo, the colt had not been sired by Basil.

Basil's behavioral history prior to coming to the Wild Animal Park in October 1982 was favorable. At his previous home, the Marwell Zoological Park in England, he sired and was present at the birth of 48 foals. He had shown no aggressive tendencies toward any of those babies.

Confused by Basil's seemingly inconsistent behavior, researchers have been able to piece together a theory on wild stallion behavior—when one wild stallion displaces another stallion as leader of a band of mares, the new stallion often kills any newborn offspring he did not sire. The fact that Basil may have killed both unrelated colts at the Wild Animal Park, yet is quite calm around Vasiliy, supports this theory of infanticide in wild horses. This breakthrough in behavioral research for wild horses enables zoos and wildlife preserves to better manage changing herds of horses.

The Przewalski's horse is extinct in the wild, and the future of the species is entirely dependent on human management. Dr. Oliver A. Ryder, geneticist for the Zoological Society of San Diego, is the species coordinator for the Przewalski's Horse Species Survival Plan and was instrumental in the 1982 exchange of Przewalski's horses between the United States and the Soviet Union.

Vasiliy's birth represents the introduction of two valuable bloodlines into the United States—Vata's and Basil's. According to Ryder, "The addition of the two new bloodlines into the gene pool helps ensure the genetic variability and stability of the Przewalski species for years to come."

# The Saga of the Tahitian Lories

## By Arthur C. Risser, Ph.D.

*Tahitian lories are small parrots, extremely rare— and, in the case reported by Dr. Art Risser, general curator of ornithology, illegal aliens. Before it was over, the caper of the hot birds had put two smugglers in jail and lories on death row.*

**June 1978**

It was late on a Sunday afternoon, October 2, 1977, when I received a call from the Security Office notifying me of three visitors, "They're interested in birds and want to ask you some questions."

And indeed they were interested in birds!

Through an interpreter who said she was a French-Canadian, the two men, one from New Caledonia and the other from Tahiti, expressed a desire to obtain the names of several aviculturists and avicultural organizations in Southern California from whom they might be able to acquire birds for their private collection.

After providing them with a reference sheet of bird societies and the names of a few local bird fanciers, I casually asked, with tongue in cheek, if they were trying to peddle "hot birds" (birds illegally brought into this country).

"Oh, certainly not," I was assured. Their major interest was just to get acquainted with the private collectors so that they might be able to exchange birds.

The next day I was contacted by one of the aviculturists whose name I had provided. "Hey, what do you know about two guys offering Tahitian lories? They called yesterday and offered to sell these birds for $7,000 a pair! I didn't know there were any in the country. They must have been smuggled in."

Later that day, reports were received that the other aviculturists on the list also had been contacted with similar offers of these rare birds, the Tahitian lories, beautiful minute parrots, about seven inches long, slightly smaller than lovebirds.

Customs agents were notified and closed in on the smugglers at a Torrance parking lot. At their trial, the smugglers pleaded guilty and were sentenced.

However, the birds became entangled in red tape. Government agencies involved each thought they should have jurisdiction over the case. United States Department of Agriculture regulations require that all birds entering the country be quarantined for a minimum of 30 days in a federally approved quarantine station to prevent the domestic poultry industry and the large avicultural collections from disease. Smuggled birds which have not met the quarantine requirements are destroyed.

Customs officials, who legally had custody of the confiscated birds, sought an exemption to the destruction rule because of the rarity of the Tahitian lories. Customs officials also had to find a place to keep their precious birds. The San Diego Wild Animal Park agreed to take the birds into quarantine while their fate was decided.

Dr. James Dolan, general curator at the Park, said, "Tahitian lories are rare, so rare, in fact, that there is a real threat that they will be extinct in a few years."

The introduction of the harrier, a hawk that feeds on small animals, and a mosquito that carries avian malaria probably has caused the disappearance of the Tahitian lory from many of the islands on which it once flourished, including Tahiti.

The media in this country, Canada and Mexico for several weeks carried the story of the plight of the Tahitian lories. Public opinion that was generated probably had immeasurable impact on the final decision. Shortly, a court order from the U.S. Attorney General's office was issued demanding that the birds be kept alive to use as evidence in the smuggling case.

For nearly a month government officials debated the question of the birds' custody and ultimate fate—resulting in the decision that the smuggled lories could be quarantined at the home of Rosemary Low, a noted lory expert, in suburban London.

Meanwhile, a second group of Tahitian lories was confiscated on January 25, 1978— from some of the same smugglers who were involved in the first attempt. It was agreed that the birds would not be killed but would be sent to Honolulu from Los Angeles to be quarantined at the government station there.

The birds were placed on exhibit at the San Diego Zoo on May 3, 1978. The birds legally remain the property of Customs but are being placed in trust at the Zoo. Our hope is that the birds will reproduce and that their offspring may be sent to other zoos to establish additional breeding groups.

*The Tahitian blue lory.*

# The Return of the Unicorn

## By James M. Dolan, Jr., Ph.D.

*The Arabian oryx, believed to be the real-life model for the mythical unicorn, was nearly hunted out of existence in its native habitat. An international conservation organization, a group of hunters and several zoos, San Diego among them, stepped in to save the oryx from extinction. General curator of mammals James Dolan describes the rescue effort.*

**February 1973**

*Arabian oryx roam the rocky hillsides of the Wild Animal Park.*

**M**illions of years ago there evolved in Eurasia a group of impressive antelopes known as the hippotragines. For some inexplicable reason this tribe deserted the land of its nativity and wandered across the Sinai to the African continent. Only one tribe member remained on the Asiatic mainland—the Arabian oryx.

As far as the written word is concerned, the oryx has been known for thousands of years, for the unicorn of the Bible is nothing other than the little oryx of the Arabian peninsula.

This species would appear to have ranged throughout most of the Middle East. About 1800, it was still found in virtually all of the Arabian peninsula, the Sinai, Lower Palestine, Transjordania, and much of Iraq. Towards the middle of the 19th Century, the oryx became rare in the northern portions of its range. By 1914, only a few oryx seemed to have survived

outside of Saudi Arabia. With the increase of human activity in the deserts and the availability of firearms due to the First World War, most of the remaining oryx in the northern population were destroyed.

By the mid-1930's the only remaining populations were found in the Nafud Desert in northern Saudi Arabia and in the Rub al Khali (Great Sandy, Empty Quarter) in the south. With the coming of oil money and automobiles, the wild populations of the Arabian oryx were doomed. In the early 1950's, as many as 300 vehicles were used in a single hunt. It was only a matter of a few years before the entire northern population was exterminated. The last oryx tracks were seen in the Nafud in 1954.

At that point the range of the oryx was confined to the extreme south of the Rub al Khali. Among Arabic people, it is believed that by eating the meat of the oryx a bullet can be expelled from the body, and to kill an oryx, which is an animal of great strength and endurance, is a sign of manhood. While this cultural policy would not seriously affect a wild population when the hunting was done from camelback, the advent of motorized transportation sounded the death knell for the oryx in the wild.

The Fauna Preservation Society in cooperation with the Survival Service Commission of the International Union for the Conservation of Nature and Natural Resources (IUCN) initiated a plan for the capture of Arabian oryx to place them in a suitable captive environment. Hopefully, they would propagate there. In 1962, an expedition was undertaken to Aden where two males and a female were captured. These animals were quarantined in Kenya and then in Europe from where they were brought to the Phoenix Zoological Garden.

The original three wild-caught animals were augmented by a female presented by the London Zoological Society. A third female was acquired in September, 1963, from the ruler of Kuwait. An additional four animals were presented by the ruler of Saudi Arabia. This then formed the breeding nucleus for the world herd of Arabian oryx in Phoenix.

After the establishment of the Phoenix herd, three animals from Saudi Arabia were imported to the Los Angeles Zoo. Both groups have done extremely well. The Phoenix herd has grown to over 30 animals and that in Los Angeles to more than a dozen. There are now slightly over 40 animals in captivity in North America, the only captive population outside the Arabian peninsula where somewhat in excess of 30 animals are also maintained in captivity. This may well represent the entire existent population.

The Zoological Society of San Diego was asked to participate in this program. An agree-

ment was reached for the transfer of six animals to the San Diego Wild Animal Park. This group consisting of four males and two females arrived on November 15, 1972.

*The legendary unicorn.*

## By Suzanne Strassburger

*In five years the oryx captive breeding program at the Wild Animal Park had proved so successful that it was possible to return the first of the rare antelope to its former range. Suzanne Strassburger, then the Park's public relations coordinator, recounts the long voyage home.*

### June 1978

The cockpit of a United Airlines cargo plane is hardly the place one would expect to find a keeper from the Wild Animal Park. Yet that is exactly the spot where Larry Schiffer was seated February 15, 1978, on the first leg of a nearly 15,000-mile trip to the Middle East and back.

Four male Arabian oryx—Fari, Halim, Aziz and Amir—were being sent to Jordan from the Wild Animal Park in the first phase of a program to reintroduce this extremely rare animal into its native land. This creamy white antelope with long ridged horns once roamed most of Arabia and the Sinai Peninsula. Now, fewer than 200 exist in only four captive breeding herds in the western hemisphere—at the San Diego Wild Animal Park; the Phoenix Zoo in Arixona; the Gladys Porter Zoo in Brownsville, Texas; and at the Los Angeles Zoo.

The Royal Jordanian Society for the Conservation of Nature maintains the Shaumari Wildlife Reserve, about 70 mi. from Amman, the capital of Jordan. It was to this 5,500 acre tract of land in the Syrian Desert that the oryx were bound.

Larry Schiffer was selected to accompany the animals because he had been working with Arabian oryx at the Wild Animal Park since 1974 as the herd grew from just six animals which arrived in 1972 from Phoenix to the 42 animals at the Park today. A total of 28 Arabian oryx have been born in San Diego since 1972.

In mid-February space became available aboard a United Airlines cargo plane from Los Angeles to New York. Larry, other keepers, and Park veterinarians prepared the oryx for the long flight to Jordan. Each animal, with his long graceful horns covered by rubber tubing to prevent their being broken, was carefully loaded into his own wooden crate designed with circular air vents and sliding doors. Sudan hay was placed inside the crate for the animals to eat during their journey.

The flight was scheduled to depart at 11 p.m. Five hours later, Larry and his charges landed in New York to be greeted by cold and snow.

Larry and the oryx were transferred to United's indoor cargo area where they waited the entire day for the Royal Jordanian Airlines (ALIA) flight to Jordan. For ten hours Larry sat with the oryx, feeding them and giving them water, explaining to inquisitive airlines personnel what he was doing with four crated antelope with rubber tubing on their horns!

At 10 p.m., February 16, Larry and the oryx were finally aboard ALIA's 747 flight to Amman. "I was told the flight was supposed to be non-stop to Amman but, about midway, it was announced we were to stop in Rome, and all passengers had to disembark. Security was tight. After an hour, we were allowed to re-board along with about a hundred Jordanians departing from Rome."

It was dark when the ALIA flight touched down in Amman on February 17. While Larry was expedited through customs, the oryx were loaded into a five-ton army truck. Larry said, "No one there could believe how large the oryx were, since they had seen only pictures of them until then. I guess the Jordanians wanted to be ready for any contingency, so that's why such a large truck was ordered."

About a two-hour journey from Amman lay the Shaumari Wildlife Reserve, in Azraq National Park.

"I was surprised to see how flat it was in the desert. It was also cold, and the wind seemed to go right through me," said Larry. "However, my first concern was the welfare of the Arabian oryx, so despite the long flight and the jeep trip, we unloaded the oryx into their new pens."

Larry was up early the next morning, as were the two Jordanian keepers assigned to the reserve. Their first task was to clean the enclosures, since the oryx were the first inhabitants of Shaumari. Larry also made it his responsibility to check all the fences and locks.

Earlier, a decision had been made to keep the male oryx in their enclosures at Shaumari until female oryx could join them and a breeding herd was established. Larry said, "If the animals were released into the Azraq National Park, there's no assurance against a hole being poked in the fence, and then the animals might escape."

As Larry expected, Halim, Fari, Aziz and Amir took one look at their new enclosures in

*Arabian oryx from San Diego get acquainted with their new home in Jordan. Photo by J.F. Clarke, WWF*

*One keeper distracts the oryx, while another places food in his pen. Photo by J.F. Clarke, WWF*

Jordan and began bouncing off the fences.

"Halim, who is only one and one-half years old, was particularly jumpy," Larry explained. "I didn't want him to injure himself, so I decided to walk into his enclosure and literally stand in his path. Halim came within three feet of me, then stopped short. He knew I wasn't going to move."

From then on, the oryx settled into their new surroundings. They even allowed the Jordanian keepers to approach, and Larry began teaching the Jordanians how to care for the animals.

"Needless to say, word was out fast in surrounding villages that some strange, new animals had come to Shaumari. The villagers were curious. But even more curious was a veterinarian from Amman who arrived with his family. He had, of course, never seen an Arabian oryx before. He thought he could just

walk up to an oryx and examine it, as he would a dog or cat. So, you can imagine how disappointed he was when I told him that only keepers and a veterinarian assigned to the reserve were allowed into the enclosures.

"Over there, my word was law concerning the welfare of the oryx!"

By mid-March, the Arabian oryx were fully acclimated to their new surroundings and the Jordanian keepers were capable of caring for the animals.

Exactly one month after his departure from San Diego, Larry came back, completing the unprecedented job of returning a rare desert antelope to its native land.

# Cheetahs

**By Helena Fitch**
**Susan Millard**
**Richard Tenaza, Ph.D.**

*The cheetah, the world's fastest land mammal, is fast heading toward extinction in the wild. The Zoo has attempted to preserve the famed hunting cat through captive breeding since 1970. Successes, failures and future prospects are related by behaviorist Helena Fitch, research assistant Susan Millard and University of Pacific professor Richard Tenaza.*

**May 1985**

"When the cheetah lived in India, it lived most commonly in low rugged hills, and came down from its lair amidst rocks and boulders to hunt in the neighbouring plains. It hunted gazelle and antelope, and probably smaller animals and birds."

This quote from S.H. Prater's *Book of Indian Animals* paints a melancholy picture. The Indian cheetah lives no longer in those rugged hills, for it is extinct. The last wild Indian cheetah was shot in 1948, and the final captive specimen died in the Mysore Zoo in the 1960's.

Cheetahs once lived in North America and Europe, and in Asia and Africa. The American and European forms are known only as fossils, Asian cheetahs may already be extinct and, to quote cheetah researcher Randal Eaton, the African cheetah is "racing to extinction."

It is estimated that between 10,000 and 24,000 cheetahs live in Africa. Their numbers are declining, partly because of hunting and poaching, but mainly because of human encroachment on their habitat.

To help prevent extinction of this spectacular cat, the Zoological Society of San Diego has undertaken a cheetah breeding program. This has resulted in 48 cheetah births at the Wild Animal Park since 1970.

Such breeding in zoos can ensure the survival of cheetahs, even if they become extinct in the wild. Because of Federal import restrictions, it is nearly impossible to bring more cheetahs into the United States, even from places in Africa where they are hunted as vermin. Consequently, captive breeding programs must rely on individuals already at hand.

The cheetah, known as the world's fastest land mammal, has been clocked at speeds up to 70 miles per hour, much faster than a race horse, though it cannot run as far.

*The cheetah in repose.*

The cheetah's long, slender legs, greyhound-like torso, and doglike claws contribute to its speed. Cheetahs catch prey by running it down at high speed in broad daylight. With rare exceptions, cheetahs do not hunt at night. Running 60 or 70 miles per hour in the dark would be dangerous and foolhardy, and Nature did not design the cheetah foolishly.

One of the cheetah's hunting techniques is to move in full view toward a large herd of gazelles or other antelope until they scatter and run. If any animal in the herd shows a weakness, such as a limp, or if it moves more slowly than the rest, the cheetah singles it out and the chase is on. If, on the other hand, all in the herd appear capable of escaping, the hunt is abandoned.

When the prey consists of a single animal or small herd, a stalking technique is used. With use of available ground cover, the cheetah cautiously approaches until it is close enough to overtake its victim with one burst of speed. Whatever technique is used, the cheetah always focuses on a single individual, ignoring all others.

The cheetah brings down a gazelle or other antelope either by hooking it with the strongly curved dew claw, or by tripping it. Prey is usually gripped by the throat and suffocated, though smaller animals may be killed by a bite at the nape of the neck.

After making a kill, the cheetah is often so overheated and exhausted that it must rest 30 minutes before eating. When the cheetah finally feeds, it does so rapidly. If a lion, hyena, or leopard comes along, it will drive the cheetah off and consume the prey. Leopards and lions have also been known to kill and eat cheetahs.

Ironically, the cheetah's spectacular hunting prowess so fascinated man that these animals were captured for use in sport hunting, contributing to the species' demise in India, Persia, and Arabia. Asian cheetah populations were decimated by the 19th century, and attempts at captive breeding were unsuccessful. To perpetrate the sport in Asia, cheetahs eventually had to be imported from East Africa.

The first cheetah exhibited in Europe was housed at the London Zoo in 1829. The United

*The cheetah
aroused.*

States began exhibiting cheetahs in 1871 in
New York's Central Park Zoo. Most of the
early captive specimens were of East African
origin, but by the 1960s, the emphasis shifted
to importation of cheetahs from southwest
Africa. Nearly all the captive cheetahs alive
today originated from southwest Africa.

The San Diego Zoo received its first
cheetah in 1933 from the explorers Martin and
Osa Johnson. During the next 37 years, 17
cheetahs were exhibited at the Zoo.

The first cheetahs to be born in captivity
were born at the Philadelphia Zoo in 1956,
but they did not survive. In 1960, a litter
was born at the Krefeld Zoo in Germany,
and the cubs were successfully hand-raised.
In 1966, cheetahs were born in Luciano
Spinelli's private collection outside Rome.
These were the first two recorded instances
of captive-born cheetahs being successfully
raised by the mother.

In 1970, the Zoological Society of San
Diego initiated a breeding program with
five pairs of adult cheetahs imported from
Namibia. Housed in a large, off-exhibit area
at the San Diego Wild Animal Park, this
colony produced its first litter on November
22, 1970. By 1976, 7 litters with a total of 31
cubs had been born.

During the next six years, only one litter
was born at the Wild Animal Park and none of
those cubs survived. The breeding animals in
the collection had been captured as adults and
may have passed reproductive age during this
time. Most of the cubs from earlier litters had
been sold or traded to other zoos, and most of
those that remained proved infertile.

Animal Behaviorist Don Lindburg took
charge of the cheetah breeding project in 1981.
Each cheetah in our collection was evaluated
for breeding potential, and trades and breeding
loans were arranged with other zoos.

Consequently, five litters, with a total of 14
cubs, have been born at the Wild Animal Park
since 1982. All but 5 of the 12 surviving cubs
have been sent to other zoos to fulfill breeding
loan agreements. By sharing breeding adults
and their offspring, zoos minimize the problems
of inbreeding and of finding compatible mates
for potential breeding animals.

Today, the cheetah's survival may depend
on the success of captive breeding projects. In
some parts of Africa, wild cheetahs are still
shot as vermin, and their skins are often sold
to tourists. The Zoological Society's successful
cheetah breeding program and cooperative programs involving other zoos provide hope that
the world's fastest land mammal has a future.

*(preceding page)*
*King vulture*
*(Sarcoramphus*
*papa)*

*(above) Gang-*
*gang cockatoos*
*(Callocephalon*
*fimbriatum)*

*(lower left) Red-*
*tailed hawk*
*(Buteo*
*jamaicensis)*

*(lower right)*
*Pesquet's parrot*
*(Psittrichas*
*fulgidus)*

*(above) Brown
pelican
(Pelecanus
occidentalis)*

*(below) Caribbean
flamingos
(Phoenicopterus
ruber ruber)*

*(following page)
Scarlet-chested
grass parrakeet
(Neophema
splendida). Photo
by R. Van
Nostrand*

# Building a Dream

## By James M. Dolan, Jr., Ph.D.

*In 1972, 56 years after its birth, the Zoo opened a second campus. The Wild Animal Park's ambigious concept: to establish a breeding reserve in which large herds of animals, many endangered species, could roam secure and reproduce their kind. On the Park's 10th anniversary one of its prime movers recalls the dream and how it grew.*

**November 1981**

As in all things, with the exception of Genesis, the beginning is usually inauspicious. And so it was ten years ago with the San Diego Wild Animal Park, although the dreams were great.

In concept and form, the Wild Animal Park was the first installation of its kind to be undertaken by an already established North American zoological society. Blessed with a mild climate, a progressive organization, and an understanding and supportive public, a spacious open air zoological park could become a reality.

The stimulation to establish a second campus in San Diego was provided by the rapid decline of wild animal populations and the accelerated destruction of wild areas. The old zoo concepts for managing large animal species had to be put aside and new methods for their husbandry undertaken if long term, self-sustaining populations were to be established as safeguards against extinction.

Such a goal could not hope to achieve the necessary success where only two or three individuals of a given species could be accommodated. Genetic diversity would be greatly reduced, which could ultimately lead to the collapse of the entire project. With this in mind, the design for the Wild Animal Park was so planned that generous land areas would be

*Moonrise over the Wild Animal Park.*

available, enabling, in gregarious species, the establishment of herds of at least 40 individuals.

The foundation for those species chosen to be exhibited would be as broad based as possible to ensure maximum genetic input. Acquisition by import would seem to be a relatively simple problem, as captive stocks of numerous antelopes and other hoofed animals can be found in collections around the world.

Unfortunately, the Wild Animal Park was not approved as a permanent quarantine facility, as are the San Diego Zoo and other major North American zoos. In essence, that meant that only hoofed mammals from countries free

*Two who brought the dream to life: Anderson Borthwick, former Zoological Society president (left) and Dr. Charles R. Schroeder, executive director emeritus.*

of hoof-and-mouth disease could be considered when stocking the Wild Animal Park.

Acceptable countries, other than the United States, included Canada, Japan, Australia, New Zealand, and Finland. As Australia and New Zealand had long had legislation prohibiting the importation of hoofed animals, those two countries could not be considered as prime sources of supple. Finland has only one major zoo, which specializes primarily in winter-hardy species, not especially suited to the California climate. Japan was just beginning to build exotic collections of her own, and Canada could not supply the diversity of species desired because of her own import regulations and the housing requirements imposed by her climate. The final solution was to contact our sister institutions in the United States.

For several years, surplus stock was retained at the San Diego Zoo in anticipation of the construction of holding facilities in the San Pasqual Valley. This was no easy task, as it tied up most of the holding facilities in an already crowded collection. Fortunately, it was possible to begin moving animals to San Pasqual in 1969.

Between 1969 and 1971, an intensive acquisition program was undertaken. Fortunately, large stocks of antelopes were available from institutions in the United States although deer were, and still are, poorly represented in North American collections.

Whereas cloven-hoofed animals could not be imported, this prohibition did not extend to elephants, rhinos, tapirs, horses, zebras, and asses, as these species do not carry hoof-and-mouth disease or rinderpest.

After some negotiation with the South African government, it was possible to purchase 20 young southern white rhinoceroses, which arrived on February 17, 1971. The southern white rhino had been on the

*San Pasqual Valley before the Park was built.*

*The Wild Animal Park under construction.*

*The Wild Animal Park's Nairobi Village.*

verge of extinction in the early 1930s, but because active conservation measures were taken by the South Africans, the population had increased to the point that the surplus was being offered for export.

At the time of arrival of the group of 20, only a single calf had ever been conceived and born in captivity, and this in South Africa. The first San Diego calf was born in October, 1972, from a cow received in February, 1971, sired by the now famous San Diego bull, Mandhla. Mandhla, to date, has been the father of 42 calves, the largest number of white rhinos born outside of Africa. Due to the success of the South African conservation program and the efforts being made with this magnificent animal, it has been removed from the endangered list.

Besides the white rhinoceros, black and Indian rhinoceros were also acquired for the collection, as both species are desperately in

need of captive propagation. Both have subsequently bred.

The major thrust was, and continues to be, the formation of breeding units of endangered species. Therefore, we accepted the invitation to join the breeding consortium, called the World Herd, for Arabian oryx.

This beautiful antelope from the deserts of Arabia was extinct in the wild by the early 1970s. The major early work in its captive propagation was undertaken by the Arizona Zoological Society, in Phoenix. It is from the Phoenix group that the Wild Animal Park herd was originally derived.

Reproduction has been so successful here that animals have been sent to Tierpark Berlin, Zurich, Rotterdam, Israel, Rabat, Shaumari Reserve, Jordan, the New York Zoological Society's conservation center at St. Catherine's Island, Georgia, and most importantly to Oman. The last known wild oryx were seen in

*Rhinos roam the plains much like their African homeland.*

*Visitors and local residents: a summer night's train ride.*

*Okapi.*

Oman in 1972, and the present effort will introduce San Diego-born animals into the species' former habitat. This is the goal in the propagation of endangered species—to place them back into the natural state.

A major effort at present is the breeding of okapis, the forest-living relatives of the giraffe. The beautiful okapi is native to the humid forests of Zaire, where its export is prohibited. In North America there are only seven females distributed in three collections. Two of the females are at the Wild Animal Park. What is so unusual about this project is that the two females belong to other zoos—the Chicago Zoological Park at Brookfield, Illinois and the Cheyenne Mountain Zoo at Colorado Springs. It is in the interest of propagation and the continuance of the species in North America

that these two zoos were prepared to send such valuable animals to the Wild Animal Park, where they could be bred to an unrelated male. The Cheyenne Mountain female has already produced one calf, and her second is due. It is our hope that there will be a successful birth from the Chicago female in 1982.

From a rather meager beginning, the San Diego Wild Animal Park has grown to be the largest collection of hoofed mammals ever assembled, with 93 species and subspecies. Furthermore, the reproduction success is unequaled in the world. Although the major emphasis has been on the ungulates, gorillas play an important park in the conservation effort of this park. These gentle forest primates are in grave danger of extinction, and every effort must be made to preserve them in captivity. Three successful births have occurred here, and the breeding male, Trib, is the father of two additional youngsters born in other collections to females who have honeymooned in San Diego.

The past 10 years have been a wonderful experience for all who are connected with the Wild Animal Park; we have watched it grow and have been thrilled by its success. But the best is yet to come.

# Who Needs Wild Animals?

## By Sheldon Campbell

*The preservation of the other life forms with whom we share the earth is not something we owe them. Rather, as Sheldon Campbell forcefully argues, it is something we owe ourselves—because, without wild animals, we are lost.*

**November 1979**

Given what we know about the growth of human population—a projected 11,500,000 by the year 2050 and knowing the unmistakable correlation between increased human population and the extinction of animal species since 1650, unavoidable confrontations between men and wild animals in the future will further accelerate rates of extinction.

Over and over, the conflicts—between Indian farmers and Gir lions, Wyoming ranchers and golden eagles, railroad builders in Tanzania and Serengeti antelope, lumbermen in Indonesia and Sumatran rhino, tuna fishermen and porpoises, and thousands more—will occur as competition increases for the remaining living space and the last of earth's resources.

But the confrontations will be on the periphery of the human mass. At center, paradoxically, people will experience greater separation, both physically and psychologically, from wilderness and wildlife. Most human beings will live in monster cities with 10 to 25 million people. To these, so far removed from wilderness, wild animals will become abstractions, pictures in books, with no more reality than visitors from Mars.

At present, half of the earth's available energy, mostly from plants, is consumed by human beings—which means, obviously, that all

*Dawn over the Wild Animal Park: a new hope?*

*Sisquoc, first California condor to be successfully reared in captivity.*

the rest of the animal kingdom must content themselves with the remainder. And in every developing nation the citizens expect that someday they or their children will have a standard of living comparable to those in developed nations like the United States.

When people continue to have such rising expectations and they appear to be thwarted by competing wildlife—as the hungry elephant may compete with the Kikuyu farmer for his corn, or the nesting tern hinders the further recreational use of San Diego's Mission Bay—they will be inclined to ask: WHO NEEDS WILD ANIMALS?

Once we would not have needed to answer the question. Over most of the 3.6 million years that hominids have walked upright across the earth, we and the rest of wildlife were inseparable, and we understood that the animals were indispensible to us.

Our lives as villagers and later city dwellers began a mere 240 to 300 generations ago (8,000 to 10,000 years) of the more than 108,000 generations we have been humankind. With the beginning of villages began the separation of men from wild animals, slowly at first, but at an accelerating rate as we changed our relationships with the ecosystems of which we had so long been a part.

Before the separation began, our most pressing need for wild animals was obvious. Some of them provided most of our food, some tools, and later, enabled us to live in colder climates by providing clothing.

Unlike the other anthropoids, our forefathers moved out of the thick forests into the open savannah country where most of the game animals lived. We were omnivores, but we soon developed a greater appetite for meat than our nearest primate relatives, and apparently we went to the places where the greatest amount of meat could be found.

It was a significant move, for in earning our living as hunters, we began and continued the process of developing and honing our brains.

We were predators, hunters of evasive game. Evolution has many rules, and one of them is that predators must be smarter than the animals they stalk, or they won't survive. Studies of the ratio of brain size to body weight provide a key to intelligence which shows that predators invariably have a higher ratio than their principal prey.

But here enters another rule of evolution. The *status quo* is never maintained. It never, in fact, exists. If predators are much smarter than their prey, then the prey gets wiped out. Consequently, the prey animals become sharper witted in order to avoid being eaten and the predators continue to get smarter in order to eat.

Put in stark terms, then, we needed the wild animals around us for food and clothing, and as it turned out, we needed them to develop our brain.

How long it took us to develop our prowess as hunters, nobody knows. At first we may have obtained our meat by scavenging the kills of other predators or by the capture of small animals like rabbits or baby antelope. Possibly the first cooperative hunters developed a single tribe and through their cooperation achieved an enormous competitive advantage over neighboring tribes.

We know that our hominid ancestors came early to the use of tools as an aid in hunting. They made simple hand-held stone axes at first, which they could use to achieve devastating effects.

Sometime during the latter part of those 100,000 generations we were hunters, we found another reason why we needed animals. We took wild dogs, previously our competitors, and made them tame. In the dog, our first domesticated animal, we really developed another tool for hunting, but we also found a companion. As part of the hunting band, dogs provided an invaluable extension of our human senses, for their sense of smell was much more acute than ours. They could track game that otherwise we had no hope of following.

But neither the technology nor the ability to see conceptually the usefulness of the dog would have been possible had our ancestors not evolved the use of language, and because of language, abstract thought.

Animals were among the first objects we gave names to. To each we assigned a specific designation, for it was critically important to us that we differentiated them one from the other, not only in relation to obtaining our food and clothing, but also in knowing animals we had to avoid because they would kill us.

*Arabian oryx at the Wild Animal Park, a conservation success story.*

What started the development of language, the chief way we differentiate ourselves from other animals, we cannot say. But we could not have developed and refined it without the vast world of wild animals which surrounded us. Without them, in short, we would not have learned to think, nor to do something no other animals can do—pass along our history from generation to generation through the use of words.

As we used wild creatures to hone our predator's brain, build our vocabularies, and develop our unique ability to use conceptual thought, so also from the attributes we saw in animals, we learned and taught our children more about ourselves. It was no accident that most children's stories use—and continue to use—animal characters, often playing human roles.

In cave paintings, carved ivory figures, and other expressions of the first human art, some students have seen also the beginnings of religion. Theories of creation are as important to any religion as theories of an afterlife, and in virtually all religions, animals are indispensible. The animals chosen for worship either carried some obvious attribute such as great strength or, more often, characteristics which to our ancestors seemed not of this world or difficult to explain except by magic, or the existence of gods.

Two other aspects of our ancestors' need for animals are closely related to the use of animals in religion. All early medicine was a combination of compounds, incantation and magic, and a dash of prayer. Most compounds came from either plants or animal parts, particularly the horns of deer, antelope, and

*ZOONOOZ ad from the '30s: acceptable then but not now.*

rhinos, ground to a powder and taken internally for various ailments or used as an aphrodisiac.

While it was characteristic of our hunting ancestors to respect all animals, even the ones they killed, they respected some more than others for religious reasons, and they believed some to be leagued with evil forces, or the ghosts of departed dead.

Other animals were thought to be unclean, and unfit for human consumption. Particular animals therefore became taboo. For any species deemed taboo, no greater protection could exist. No harm could befall them. Many taboos are still with us. Today in the largely Muslim country of Senegal, West Africa, wart hogs, considered untouchable by Muslims, prosper and propagate while touchable antelope perish under the poacher's gun.

Our interaction with the rest of the animal kingdom has been indispensible to our own evolution. What we are today in language, intelligence, and the capacity for conceptualizing abstract ideas, we could not have achieved without that interaction over thousands upon thousands of generations. Nor would we have achieved it without the great diversity of animal forms that we encountered; had the forms been few we would have had no need for the many convolutions that enable our highly evolved brains to hold more information than the most sophisticated computer.

Wild animals supplied the greatest part of our food and clothing, and many of our tools, for most of the time hominids have existed on earth. Only in recent times, the last eight to ten thousand years, did we turn to agriculture for the bulk of our food supply, and ironically by so doing enabled ourselves to depart from the condition that limited population growth in hunter-gatherer societies, namely a food supply over which we had no control, and that established the number of men that could live in any particular area.

While many people acknowledge our vast unpaid debt to the rest of the animal kingdom, some apparently now believe that we can continue to cause the extinction of other species without bringing harm to ourselves—as though humankind and the rest of nature had become two distinct entities.

The greatest impetus to separation from the wild in what are now called the developed nations, came with the Industrial Revolution and the rapid growth of large cities, railroads, and highways. Increasingly, country folk left their farms to find work in the cities, thereby losing touch with wild animals, except for those in zoos.

Both industrialism and increased farm pro-

*The giant panda: among the most endangered.*

duction encouraged human population to soar in a process that began to feed on itself as burgeoning populations created new markets for greater production.

Up until recently this process was called PROGRESS, and wild animals often stood in the way of PROGRESS. When they did, they were eradicated. If any remained—like the 89 bison left alive in the United States at the turn of the century—they lived in small pockets of their former range. The same process is now being repeated in all the developing nations.

If one does not see wild animals, does not in many cases know that they exist, they cannot seem important. One may support conservation as an indulgence, but without any conviction that wild animals are really indispensible to us or the future of the world.

A few voices warn that we still have much to gain, just as we have always gained from wild creatures. Unless people have the arrogance to believe they can control their own evolution, without regard to the rest of nature, they should desperately try to keep alive all wild animal forms they are now driving rapidly towards extinction.

Nobody knows, nor can anybody foresee, what roles these forms may play in our future—that decision will be made by evolution—but we will surely need them. In our continual tinkering with nature it would be best to follow Aldo Leopold's first rule of intelligent tinkering—*save all the parts.*

# INDEX